Reading th

The Ultimate Guide to the Rider Waite Tarot Cards

Reading the Tarot

The Ultimate Guide to the Rider Waite Tarot Cards

The #1 Workbook for Learning How to Read Tarot Cards, Tarot Card Meanings, and Simple Tarot Spreads to Get You Started

Shawna Blood

Reading the Tarot – The Ultimate Guide to the Rider Waite Tarot Cards

Published by CAC Publishing LLC

ISBN: 978-1-950010-23-3 paperback

ISBN: 978-1-950010-22-6 eBook

Disclaimer

This book has been written for information purposes only. Every effort has been made to make it as complete and accurate as possible, but mistakes may be present in typography or content. This book also provides information only up to the publishing date. Therefore, it should be used only as a guide, not as the ultimate source.

The purpose of this book is to educate. The author and publisher do not warrant that the information contained herein is fully complete and shall not be responsible for any errors or omissions. The author and publisher shall have neither liability nor responsibility to any person or entity with respect to any loss or damage caused or alleged to have been caused directly or indirectly by this book.

Table of Contents

Introduction

The tarot can be useful in helping you cope with pain, identifying your next steps when feeling lost or confused and can keep you on track toward your goals. When you are plagued by inertia, you can consult the tarot for a strategy plan to get yourself back on the path to success. It is also there to offer spiritual guidance in your most profound times of need.

What is the Tarot?

The Tarot consists of a deck of 78 cards that, over the centuries, absorbed the knowledge, stories, beliefs, histories, morals and life lessons of numerous cultures. Combine that with the all-powerful mind we possess, and we can use the Tarot to obtain vision into our lives, allow us to achieve, and strengthen us when we need to cope. Know that when reading the Tarot, we already know the answers to our own questions. However, those answers are concealed within our subconscious. The Tarot assists us in extracting that information.

There are 3 predominant tarot card systems which are generally used today - Marseille (around 1440), Rider-Waite-Smith (around 1909), and Thoth (around

1969). I personally like Rider-Waite-Smith and lean towards the Golden Dawn interpretive method.

Others may tell you that you don't need to know anything to read tarot. They say you can simply use your "psychic intuition". I humbly disagree. Critical theory is vital to accurately gaining a complete understanding of the Tarot.

Anatomy of a Tarot Deck

A Tarot deck has 78 cards that are divided into the **Major Arcana** which contains 22 illustrated cards numbered Key 0 to Key 21, and the **Minor Arcana** which contains 56 numbered (pip) and court cards. Some versions will not have pictures on the pip cards. Instead, they look comparable to a deck of playing cards: Ace thru Ten. The court cards consist of the Page, the Knight, the Queen, and the King. There may be, though, diverse names for the court cards, like Prince, Princess, etc. The Minor Arcana are separated into 4 suits, commonly termed Wands (which are Clubs), Cups (which are Hearts), Swords (which are Spades), and Pentacles (which are Diamonds). Other names may be used dependent upon the deck.

The Major Arcana denote universal archetypical forces which rule life. When you see the Major Arcana take over a reading, it more than likely means that great natural forces are existing. The Minor Arcana denote the various sides of the human condition. The 4 suits of the Minor Arcana largely correspond to the tables below:

WANDS

creative energy, personal or professional development
Element - Fire
Energy – Active (Yang)
Season - Spring
Class - Proletariat

CUPS

emotions, sentiments, interpersonal relationships
Element - Water
Energy – Passive (Yin)
Season - Summer
Class - Clergy

SWORDS

ambition, aggression, strife, conflict, intellectual or ideological energies
Element - Air
Energy – Active (Yang)
Season - Fall

Class - Nobility

PENTACLES

material world, finances and property, wealth, security
Element - Earth
Energy – Passive (Yin)
Season - Winter
Class – Artisans/Merchants

How does the Tarot work?

The Tarot is a tool used to generate the most probable outcome in life. That outcome, nevertheless, is never secure. This is because no one person can actually forecast the future with certainty. Why? Because we all possess the necessary willpower to change anything at any time. You are free to change your actions, attitude, words and thoughts. The Tarot serves as a guide for what needs to be changed to produce the results you want, but the concrete effort to make that change rests solely with you.

Historical Overview

Playing cards go all the way back to the Tang Dynasty in China, 618 A.D. to 907 A.D. Cultural or mythical orientations were demonstrated on the cards and used to play games. It has been told that the emperor's concubines would use the cards to tell fortunes. It is said that they did this in order to deal with the tedious boredom they felt when the emperor wasn't around. Eventually, the cards were taken to the Middle East (around 1370). They ended up in Europe.

Around 1440, a deck of 78 cards with illustrations immersed. At that time, the Tarot was a card game, typically used by the wealthy. The Church barred playing cards under anti-gambling regulations, but nonetheless, in many cases, granted exemptions for the Tarot because it was played by the influential nobles of the time.

1780 France and England holds the earliest record of the Tarot being used for prediction where they used a deck known as the "Tarot de Marseille".

A listing of main occultist players who rose to distinction as tarot scholars:

- Eteilla (1790s)

- Eliphas Levi (1850s)

- Encausse, known by his penname Papus (1890s)

- members of the Hermetic Order of the Golden Dawn thereinafter and well through the 1900s.

Thereafter, in 1909, A. E. Waite created the Rider-Waite-Smith Tarot System. Rider being the first publisher. And Pamela Colman Smith, the artist. As previously stated, I am most comfortable with this system.

Nowadays there are numerous versions of Tarot, most of them pretty much the same as Rider-Waite-Smith, the Tarot de Marseille or Thoth system.

Why the Tarot Works

Let's talk about "Qi" (pronounced chee), which is known as the natural life energy that flows thru every being and cosmically links us to each another. The theory of Qi is used in old-style Chinese medicine, Feng Shui, martial arts and Taoism. Your spirit or soul is your personal Qi. It is why you are alive. Your Qi joins your physical roles to one another. Qi joins your physical purposes to your mental. And it joins your mental to your spiritual. In addition, your personal Qi is linked to every other personal Qi in the universe. That is known as "Universal Qi".

I believe in this life force known as "Qi" or the collective unconscious.

My theory is that the Tarot works when you succeed to link the reader's personal Qi with the other person's personal Qi. Then, they are liked with the Universal Qi. At that point, something really amazing happens, which some people call synchronicity, where specific cards are drawn that best answer the question asked. Incredible stuff!

Is the Tarot against your religion?

This is a question I am faced with often, so let me answer it in the best way I know how. Most conventional faiths are against fortunetelling. Let me just say that sacramental wine is still classified as drinking alcohol. Alcohol is alcohol, which possesses neither virtue nor sin. It is simply what you choose to do with it. You need a knife to0 for lots of good things, such as cutting loose a rope. A knife, however, can also be used to kill someone. Guns can be used to murder, but they can also be used to protect. There is nothing wrong with gambling, but hand the dice over to a gambling addict and there will be an issue.

Basically, whether the Tarot is against your religion or not fully depends upon how you use it. I personally find it very tough to say that the Tarot is in contradiction of the teachings of your God.

For instance, the Bible cautions against looking for seers for prophecy reasons. The way prophecy is used in the Bible is different from the way I use the word. Prophecy as used in the Bible denotes soothsaying, talking with certainty about an individual's future, talking with certainty about the resolve of the higher powers, and assuming that any human being knows what the higher powers know.

My classification of prophecy is to see and know YOURSELF with clearness, not to see or know your future or fate. The Tarot is used to aid you in making sense of YOU and ONLY YOU. And, it does not give you your future. It simply helps you to discover what the most probable result is founded on, and your present activities and attitudes. In other words, it won't tell you what you are intended to do. Rather, it helps you to understand what your weaknesses and strengths are. In my years with the Tarot as a helpful tool, I can't see how any of the conventional religions who are against Tarot could reasonably be against it.

Having said that, any individual who is going to practice the Tarot should reach a good level of maturity prior to practicing it. It is not suitable for young children as they have not achieved that yet.

The ongoing illiteracy of society when it comes to the Tarot upsets me, because that unawareness is what ruins the legitimization. I will assume that religion comes into play only to shield people from going to quacks and falling into traps. That is the only

justification that makes sense to me for being against
the Tarot.

Meanings of The Rider Waite Deck of Tarot Cards

Below you will find some suggested meanings of the Rider Waite deck of Tarot Cards. Included are the cards of the Major Arcana and the 4 Suits - Suit of Cups, Suit of Wands, Suit of Pentacles and Suit of Swords.

These meanings are intended to get you underway with understanding the cards for yourself.

Observe the colors, pictures and symbols and notice what is happening in the picture and any instantaneous feeling or reaction that you may have. This is called your "intuition" or "higher guidance".

If you find yourself disagreeing with any of my definitions, that is okay. Make note of your intuitive definitions in your "Tarot Journal". This is your own personal insight speaking to you, and as you build up your individual relationship with your cards you will use these definitions (or mine, either is fine).

Have fun!

Major Arcana

The Fool

Keywords to Use

Optimism, courage, faith, new ideas, heading into the unknown, spontaneity, childlike ambitions, letting go of expectations and feeling uninhibited and free to express yourself and to create something magical and wonderful, carefree, go with the flow, detach from worldly values and possessions, trust yourself, support of Universe, simplicity, potential of spirit, risk, leap of faith, personal quest.

Symbols

The White Dog

By tradition, in fairy tales and stories, when somebody goes on a journey, they are usually accompanied by some sort of animal.

The dog is known for attempting to warn the person about the likely imminent danger of stepping over the edge of a cliff or he could also be jumping excitedly by his side, encouraging him every step of the way.

The Bag on a Stick

This signifies past experiences and memories. The person is taking with him the bare minimum that he needs. He is mindful of his possessions, but they do not control him. Taking so little on his voyage, he trusts that he will be provided for.

Meaning

There is a chance for new beginnings. You might feel a strong longing to take a leap of faith and do something entirely different with your life. Believe in what your heart is telling you, go with the flow and let the Universe support you.

You may need to include some logic in your plans, but don't use logic as a reason for not following your heart or your dreams.

The Magician

Keywords to Use

Tap into your innermost capabilities, connect with the Universe, use things that you can't see like energies, feelings and thoughts to help with the creation process.

Trust your instinct. You undoubtedly have more inner resources than you give yourself credit for. Manifest, create, feel the power, ground it and then turn it into something useful and powerful.

Colors

Yellow (emotions), red (power, strength and material) and white (spiritual)

Symbols

The Figure 8

Infinity

Snake Around Waist

Infinity

Red Roses and White Lilies

Love and Intellect

Greens

Earth

Table Symbols

cup (emotions), wand (creativity), sword (intellect) and pentacle (money)

Meaning

You have all of the abilities, talents and resources to be, do and have anything you desire in life. You might not recognize the skills you have. Trust in yourself and be your own authority. With the Magician card, you can choose a course of action and focus your attention to manifest whatever you desire.

Set the goal that everything you are manifesting and creating is derived from a place of the highest love and is for the highest good of all concerned.

Trust in yourself and your capabilities. You are capable of attracting all the people and resources you need. Believe in yourself and create magic.

The High Priestess

Keywords to Use

Secrecy, things are not all what they seem, insight, unknown, the feminine, moon, moon cycles, unseen secrecies of nature/science, power in stillness/contemplation, keep secrets, psychic, strength/feminine power, passive, open/approachable, strength through no action, standoffish, private, outwardly unemotional, innermost feelings are hidden.

Colors

Blue (emotions- cool color, represents emotions, dispassionate and disconnected), black (contrast between physical and spiritual, yin/yang male/female), white (spiritual).

Symbols

<u>The Pillars</u>

male and female- sits in the space between them – an opening or gateway.

<u>Tora</u>

5 books of Moses, book of knowledge

<u>Moon Crown</u>

Egyptian Isis Mother of Horus- moons either side and sun (Horus) in center waiting to be born, 3 phases of the moon- waxing, waning and new

<u>Pomegranates</u>

righteousness

<u>Meaning</u>

Believe in your intuition, use your inner guidance thru relaxation and meditation. Things may be hidden. It is not likely that you have all of the facts and information you need in order to make an informed decision. Ask questions to get all the information you need. One way to learn the right questions to ask is thru meditation or your dreams.

The High Priestess represents a 3rd party in a love triangle or a secret third party who has an effect on you from a distance in a business relationship.

The Empress

Keywords to Use

All is well in your life, wealth, abundant, accomplishment, creativity, productivity, maternity, pregnancy, birth, accord, fostering, at one with the earth, feminine, fertility, sensual desires, domestic solidity, fostering yourself and others, feeling and loving life thru your desires and senses.

Colors

All Colors – sense of balance and harmony Yellow – thoughts, feelings and life-giving power of the sun. Red – power and affluence. Green - nature and earth. White - spiritual

Symbols

The 12 Stars in the Crown

Symbols of the astrology

9 Pearls of the Necklace

9   planets

The Wheat

Represents abundance and is a sign of fertility

The Female

A sign of Venus - the goddess of love

The Water

The force of life and is a symbol of fertility

Pomegranates

Symbol of fertility

Meaning

Everything is expected to turn out better than you may have projected. Wealth, happiness, passion and good flow in life. You will have balance, harmony and a feeling of being nurtured and doing the nurturing.

This is a wonderful card to have come up in your spread. It can mean motherhood or pregnancy. But, it is important to first look at the other cards surrounding it prior to offering that interpretation to someone.

The Emperor

Keywords to Use

Outward power, authority, strong, justice, father figure, masculine energy, worldly power, leadership, willpower, self-control, discipline, dignified, forceful, government, traditional, stubborn, rules, contracts

Colors

Dominant Colors - Red and Orange
Red - color of the base chakra, embodies liveliness, fire, making things happen, substantial power and strength - the color of Aries – the fire sign.
Orange - authority, expert, external strength

Symbols

Egyptian Ankh

Symbol of natural life, wellbeing, contentment and immortality - total power of life and death.

The Orb and Scepter

Symbol of power and authority

Rams Heads

Sign of Aries, God of War

Long Grey Beard

Wisdom of the ages and experience

Armor

Warrior, form of defense (physical or psychological)

Meaning

Frequently means an individual with authority like a doctor or lawyer. Also means creating your physical presence and mark on the world.

It signifies outward power, strength and presence not needing to be showy about it.

Strong male energy and a father figure - someone where rules, discipline and structure are very significant and are strictly enforced on others.

The Hierophant

Keywords to Use

Innermost power, consultant, counsellor, teacher, education, pursuer of knowledge and insight, fondness for traditional and conservative, has a need to adapt and be socially accepted, priest, religious individual, religious conviction, admiration, ritual, accept punishment, judgment, skilled, belief systems, seeks a deeper meaning, honoring ritual, ceremony and tradition, part of a team or organization, likes to learn in structured groups with conventional rules and assigned procedures, sense of obedience, authority and responsibility

Colors

Regularly red – meaning power and authority. Some white – spiritual. Grey – wisdom

Symbols

<u>Two Pillars</u>

Balance/looking at both sides

<u>Crown and Scepter</u>

Triple-tiered papal crown and cross – earth, body, mind, spirit and consciousness

<u>Roses and Lilies</u>

emotion   and   logic

<u>Crossed Keys</u>

Access to secret information

<u>Hand Gesture</u>

"The Blessing" - establishing a bridge between Heaven and earth

Meaning

The Hierophant will regularly possess the role of an advisor, counsellor, teacher or expert in their field, and they will provide you with guidance. It's about developing the qualities of balance and power.

It also means dealing with your beliefs, whether religious or spiritual and being true to yourself, not blindly following the dogma of others.

The Lovers

Keywords to Use

Partnership, teamwork, connection, bond, physical, sex, desirability, love, accord, harmony, cooperation, moral choices, values

Colors

Purple - spiritual growth

Yellow - the color of your solar plexus which is your power center

Symbols

Tree of Life

Bears 12 fruits (behind the man)

Tree of Knowledge

Good and bad (behind woman)

Serpent

Means enlightenment

Archangel Raphael

Represents the superconscious mind

The unifying factor between man (logic, reason) and woman (passion, emotions)

Meaning

Indicates the more physical aspect of relationships, including intimacy and sex. May mean that a relationship is about to switch from platonic to physical.

Lovers in a relationship. In a business relationship, there may be a strong attraction between partners or coworkers.

Looking to the angels for guidance. It is a card of coming together and our desire to be connected to others in meaningful relationships.

This card echoes the importance of personal values and ethical choices. It may also represent a moral dilemma.

The Chariot

Keywords to Use

Trip, being in control, stability, focused action, willpower, self-discipline, leadership, liveliness, moving forward, charm and personality.

Colors

Yellow - the color of the sun, the solar plexus and internal power.

Blue – logic, communication, balance

Symbols

The Sphinxes

Half man/half beast - duality, yin/yang, black/white. There are two sides to everything - internal and external.

The Driver

Controlling the chariot without any reins - about the power of the mind and intense focus, especially when dealing with opposing forces, to get where you want to go in any circumstance.

Meaning

Often symbolizes travel, physically and mentally, a change of direction, and more focus being needed on the direction.

It is also about seeking help where needed and acting. Preparing for a journey, both mentally and physically.

Take control of where you want to go, and be firm and self-confident without being belligerent. Be in control of your emotions.

Strength

Keywords to Use

Internal strength, love, tenderness, compassion, faith, cooperation, harmony, consistent, bond, kind-heartedness, strength of feminine energy.

Colors

White - purity, especially spiritual

Yellow - about connecting and communicating and being in touch with who you are

Symbols

The Figure 8 - the symbol of infinity

<u>The lion</u>

Considered to be the strongest, most powerful animal, yet he is happily eating out of the woman's hand, meaning mutual trust and respect.

Meaning

Approach people and things from a soft angle. You will get much better results by using thoughtfulness, understanding, compassion, friendship and love rather than using aggression.

Do your best to see things from the viewpoint of others. Have pure intention with regard to the outcome. Avoid force. It will not work for you.

Be clear in what you want to achieve, but also be mindful of what others want to achieve, so that you can bring about a situation where everyone wins.

You have the inner strength to overcome any challenge.

The Hermit

Keywords to Use

Seclusion, separation, looking inward, reflection.

Colors

Blue and grey - dark and lonely

Symbols

The Lantern - the single light in the darkness of the rest of the card - a symbol of hope at the end of a dark tunnel

The Hermit

This card is about being on our own, through choice or sometimes by force. It is a card of refection, of looking inward, of just being with yourself away from the world.

Meaning

There is a need for some quiet time by yourself.

Reflect, get to know yourself and allow yourself to feel and experience what is going on in your life.

The light guiding you forward is offering truth and knowledge. It is also lighting your way to the place you want to go. This may be a physical or spiritual place.

A challenging card for many individuals as they are not used to simply their own company. Know that if you can make friends with yourself, you will never be lonely.

The Wheel of Fortune

Keywords to Use

Change in fortune, luck, calling, destiny, opportunity.

Colors

A mixture of all colors - a balanced card about both internal and external energies.

Symbols

The Bull, Angel, Lion and Eagle

Representing the 4 elements of Earth, Air, Fire and Water.

The letters on the wheel can be either TORA or TARO

As found on the book in the lap of the High Priestess

Wheel of Fortune

A high-energy card - things are moving fast in all areas of life. Things previously set in motion are now coming to completion. Karma - what goes around, comes around.

Meaning

New opportunities - cycles are ending and new ones are beginning.

A twist of fate could be coming, either good or challenging, depending on the neighboring cards.

Go with the flow and see what is being presented to you.

Justice

Keywords to Use

Lawful, courts, authorized, justice, fairness, balance and mediation.

Colors

Red - the color of external power.

Green - represents compassion and love, which are important in matters of justice.

Symbols

The Double-Edged Sword

Can fall in either direction. The scales of justice propose balance and fairness.

<u>Justice</u>

The individual drawing this powerful card needs to have strength and courage in whatever they are undertaking.

Meaning

A legal or official situation is near. It may have to do with mediation or negotiations.

The situation will typically turn out for the highest good. The phrase "justice will be done" applies here, although that may or may not be in favor of the person drawing this card.

It can be pointing to someone who has a good sense of justice and fairness and a vast desire to champion the underdog or support a cause they have a passion for.

There is a need to look at the situation and ask yourself whether you are being objective and balanced in your approach.

This is a card of logic. There is no place for emotion.

The Hanged Man

Keywords to Use

Postponements, patience is required, go with the flow.

Colors

Red - basic instincts

Blue – communication

Yellow - internal power and spiritual connection

Symbols

The Hanged Man

Very serene and calm, waiting for and expecting something to happen. There is a sense of contentment.

The Cross

Called a T-cross, a very old symbol. The upside-down position is called Tau, a very old meditation position.

Meaning

Postponements and delays, and the need to let go of old stuff, go with the flow and be patient.

Sometimes in life, we need to stop pushing and forcing and let matters take their own natural course.

There is an element of observation and more than likely the solutions lie in thought and meditation, rather than in busyness.

Maybe there is a need for a fresh perspective or viewpoint from the totally opposite direction. You see the world very differently when you look at it upside-down.

Death

Keywords to Use

Endings, new beginnings, change, letting go of the old.

Colors

Black and White - opposites representing positive and negative, day and night, yin and yang and duality.

Yellow - represents the dawn of new a day, new ideas and new beginnings.

Symbols

The White Rose

Also called the Mystic Rose - the symbol of life.

Meaning

This card seldom means a physical death. It is more about massive change and transformation.

Something is coming to an end, and there are much better times ahead.

Change can be extremely hard because we are moving into unknown territory and the fear of the unknown can be much harder than the familiarity of the present, even if that situation is not what we want and is not serving us.

It is painful and very difficult to let go of the past and embrace new ideas, situations and people.

It is during rough times that we learn the most about ourselves and grow the most. It likely means that it is going to be a very challenging time.

Temperance

Keywords to Use

Healing, stability, peaceful, abundantly, flow of life, tranquility, permitting, testing the waters, keeping options open.

Colors

All the Colors - balance in all areas.

There are elements of Earth (green), Air (White), Fire (Red) and Water (Blue).

The most dominant is white - suggesting spirituality, and

Red - fire connection between heaven and earth

Symbols

One Foot in the Water and One on the Land

Balance between emotions and actions.

Pouring Water Between 2 Cups

Represents the constant flow of life.

The Sun

Brings a bright new day

Meaning

Balance, moderation and pausing for thought before you act.

Temperance is a great healer of mind, body and spirit.

A card of calm, hope and optimism, and making sure you have all the facts and putting personal opinions aside.

It signifies inner strength, willpower and a quiet, knowing confidence. Take the time to listen to and feel your emotions, and do not be controlled by them.

Act when it feels like it comes from your heart and spirit.

The Devil

Keywords to Use

Obligations, agreements, excess, consequences, obsession, temptation, inner demons.

Colors

Black, white, and a lot of orange.

Meaning

This card signifies the consequences of our actions. It is frequently about fascination, excess and desire which are used harmfully or purely for self-gain.

When it comes to legal matters, this card serves as a warning to be very careful prior to taking on commitments because you may end up taking on more than you bargained for.

In relationships, it can mean that there is an obsession with material wealth and impressiveness along with other damaging things such as jealousy, greed, misuse, unkindness, need or manipulation. There is a lack of anything spiritual.

You may feel a loss of personal strength, a sense of powerlessness and that you are being controlled by someone or something else.

Know that personal power can be reclaimed and new choices can be made, or live with the consequences of decisions and actions.

If the Devil comes up, it is a clear warning NOT to do certain things you may be contemplating because the consequences are unlikely to be unpleasant.

The Tower

Keywords to Use

Disturbance, disorder, sudden change, something unforeseen.

Symbols

<u>A Stone Tower High on a Cliff</u>

Represents values, ideals and what we have created in our life.

<u>The Bolt of Lightning</u>

Represents something out of the blue which can shake our world to the core.

Meaning

Something unforeseen and unintended is happening in your life. It will possibly cause a great change and perhaps substantial turmoil. It will change what needs to change and make way for newer and better things. More than likely there have been warnings for a quite a while and the individual has not done anything about it.

It indicates a period of development and alteration, often very thought-provoking. It may be one of those events you did not see coming and could do very little to stop it anyway. Yet, you have the choice of how you react and the decisions you make to deal with this situation.

The Star

Keywords to Use

Desires, daydreams, wishes, happiness, abundantly, balance, flow.

Colors

Blue – emotions

Green - earth

Yellow - hope

Symbols

Stars

Symbols of hope and optimism

Meaning

The Star is a card of balance and abundance. It is about peace of mind, serenity, motivation – a light at the end of the tunnel - moving into better conditions.

There is also inner strength as well as playfulness – finding your way back to nature. True happiness comes from being at peace with yourself.

A reminder that the simplest of things give the greatest and most long-lasting pleasure.

Body and spirit are one, there is a lack of self-consciousness, fear and doubt. Allow yourself to enjoy the innocence of childhood.

It is the card of hopes, wishes and dreams, fulfillment in every respect of life.

The Moon

Keywords to Use

Misinterpretations, deceitfulness, lack of communication, importance of dreams, self-delusion and seeing things through rose-tinted glasses.

Symbols

Two faces on the Moon

A sign that there are at least 2 sides to the matter.

Blue Water

Representing emotions and matters of the heart.

The Moon

Associated with the Water sign Cancer, the sign of motherhood. The symbol for womanhood and a strong force in the female monthly cycle.

For men and women, it represents your feminine side, wishes, feelings and natural reactions

Meaning

The Moon signifies instinct, psychic matters and dreams, likely deceitfulness and mix-ups, possibly a need to explain matters, particularly in communication.

It can also be a card of impractical expectations and a propensity to see things through rose-tinted glasses.

You may have lost your way and are wandering around aimlessly. This card brings the promise of the unknown which can be frightening.

It can also be a time to look at things in a totally different light for the best possible outcome.

The Moon might also have to do with imagination and creativity. It can be inspirational and enthralling and hold the promise that everything your heart desires can be yours.

The Sun

Keywords to Use

Wellbeing, cheerfulness, happiness, stability, youth, health, liveliness.

Colors

Yellow - representing control, vigor, life-giving force, bravery, strength and the source of all creation.

Orange - represents physical energy and liveliness.

White - represents your spirit and an innocent sense of wonder and goodness.

Meaning

Delight, optimism, youth, poise, an innocent attitude and sense of wonder, better health and a wealth of energy, vivacity, warmth and passion.

Good physical/mental health and a positive attitude. Can show a coming back to health after a sickness.

Acknowledging your self-worth and your own capabilities. Shining radiantly and perhaps gaining importance or promotion and becoming the center of attention.

You will succeed at everything you do. It is time to let your own light shine.

Judgement

Keywords to Use

Reawakening, coming alive, courage, wake-up call, letting go of judgment of yourself and others.

Meaning

The Judgement card might show an awakening, a revelation, an unexpected awareness, great news, happiness in accomplishment.

It may also be about awakening to abilities and to the potential for greatness that each individual has inside of them. It may also be about forgiving yourself and others and letting go of negative emotions such as fault, guilt and anxiety.

There is a feeling of purging the faults of the past and starting over with new optimism. We have learned from our mistakes and are now able to move on. We are on the right path. It can also be a wake-up call, prompting us to stop hiding our greatness.

Maybe you are creating a new start and appreciating your renewed confidence. If you have a significant choice to make, it is vital to consider all the aspects and then act, without blame if it does not quite work out as you had planned.

It is important to evaluate what did not go well without feeling guilty or blaming and other damaging reproaches that frequently go with making mistakes.

The World

Keywords to Use

The world is at your feet, wholeness, accomplishment, end of a cycle.

Symbols

The 4 Symbols of the Lion

Fire

The Bull

Earth

The Eagle

Water

The Golden-Haired Man

Air

The Laurel Wreath

Success

The symbols represent a balance of all of the elements - intellect (air), emotions (water), inspiration and action (fire) and action and practicality (earth). They are the feelings of completeness, stability, wholeness and having the world at your feet.

Meaning

Integration, achievement and festivity.

You will bring to realization the outcomes of your own efforts. There is self-actualization and satisfaction with this card.

It represents your dreams coming true, having peace of mind, discovering serenity, counting your blessings, a fruitful result and things advancing into a new cycle.

Everything is working together in harmony and totality.

Minor Arcana

Suit of Cups

Ace of Cups

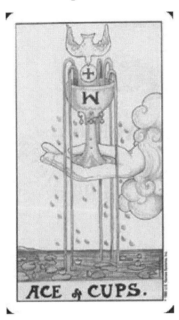

Keywords to Use

Artistic beginnings, proposal of love or friendship, innovative ideas, inspiration

Symbols

Water

Represents emotional matters.

Dove of Peace

Emotional and spiritual fulfillment.

Meaning

This card brings harmony, courage, calm, enjoyment and new emotions, love and support. It might be a new love or friendship.

It could also mean that you are relating to people in a better way and the trials of the past are moving away.

It is also the beginning of a new and exciting project.

For those who are very work and action focused, this can also be about getting in touch with your inner emotions, discovering your sensitive side, opening yourself up to others at an expressive level and believing in your intuition. Trust your profound knowing.

Because love is the spirit of this card, it may also be significant for you to look for love in all areas of your life and love yourself more. This may include empathy or compassion for yourself and/or others.

Two of Cups

Keywords to Use

Together, cooperation, partnership, soulmate

Symbols

Two People Coming Together

Union, love, friendship, partnership or blending of some type. There is frequently a deep spiritual or soul mate type of connection with this card, a feeling of mutual respect and harmony.

Meaning

The Two of Cups will often show falling in love and feelings of true connection with another individual.

This spirited connection can be an attraction, either emotionally or physically.

If this is in regard to business, it could mean friends going into business together or a new partnership where there is plenty of agreement and understanding.

There is a major amount of energy and power when 2 individuals come together in cooperation.

The Two of Cups is all about connections and closeness with other individuals in many diverse circumstances. And, it might also mean the merging of talents.

There may be one warning with this card - to ensure that there is not so much collaboration between 2 individuals that others are left out, principally in situations with friends or in business activities.

Three of Cups

Keywords to Use

Celebration, team, female friends, success.

Symbols

3 Women Holding Cups High in the Air

Celebrate.

Colors

White - spiritual purity

Yellow – energy

Orange and red - action colors

Meaning

This is a card of abundance and riches.

The Three of Cups is a card of celebration, merriment, fun and successful conclusions to projects. It can mean celebrating a special event where individuals and families come together and overlook their differences

It represents teamwork and working together successfully. It is a card of community caring and spending time with other folks.

It also signifies to the value of having female friends and your special connection with them, particularly for women. Go out and socialize.

Four of Cups

Keywords to Use

Reflection, absorption, boredom, trapped, anti-social.

Symbols

Figure Under a Tree Looking Bored

Unhappy and discontented. The three cups are offering him love, friendship and support.

The Upright Cups

Contain positive emotional experiences and he doesn't see them or he is simply choosing to ignore them.

Meaning

The Four of Cups is a card of reflection or thought and also of shutting out the rest of the world. Depending on the circumstances, this can be either a good thing or a bad thing.

In other words, it can be a positive time of self-reflection and focusing on your own emotional state. It may also indicate negative self-absorption, boredom and sadness.

Use this time for re-evaluation and search for a more inspiring existence. You may be stuck in the past and are unable to open up to new ideas, people and prospects.

Five of Cups

Keywords to Use

Loss, remorse, shame, living in the past, being let down, sadness, grief

Symbols

Figure in a Dark Cloak

He is looking at the 3 cups and the contents that have spilled out of them. He doesn't even notice the 2 upright cups behind him. This could be indicative of what is happening in your life.

Meaning

The Five of Cups is a card about looking back at events that have occurred with regret and a feeling of "If only I had...or had not done something". You are focusing on what is done or has been lost and you are therefore unable to see the good that may have come from the circumstances.

The Five of Cups is all about loss, discontent, grief, anguish and depression. You may have been emotionally let down by someone.

It can indicate going through a relationship break-up.

You may be acknowledging mistakes of the past, but are not yet ready to look forward to the future.

The surrounding cards will indicate the area of life your grief relates to.

The cards will indicate that all is not lost and that something can be recovered from the situation. There is good in everything, but it may take time and healing to see it clearly.

Six of Cups

Keywords to Use

Joyful memories, people from the past, innocent, children, inner child.

Symbols

Children in a Garden, Cups Filled with Flowers

There is cheerfulness, delight, friendship, wonder, simplicity and childlike innocence. The Six of Cups is a card of goodness that inspires you to be tender, kind, generous, empathetic and forgiving.

Meaning

The Six of Cups might be referring to the children in your life and joyful memories from childhood. It can also be that a person is coming back into your life from the past.

On its own, the Six of Cups is expected to signify someone with whom you have happy memories, though it depends upon the cards which surround it.

In romance, it could mean that an old flame will be resurfacing in your life or a current relationship that has strong roots to the past.

It may specify a need to return to a more basic life or it can show that you are possibly being a little naïve in your approach.

You might also need to look back at your youth or your inner child to discover those things that give you joy and make you happy. Maybe you need to play more.

The cards around The Six of Cups will show whether this is a positive and delightful situation or whether it is more challenging for you.

Seven of Cups

Keywords to Use

Choices, decisions, concentration, misunderstanding, mysterious.

Colors

Blue - symbolizes logic and communication

Symbols

<u>Cups</u>

An offering of many different choices which need to be regarded with emotion and logic.

Meaning

With the Seven of Cups there is much confusion and lack of focus. There are many choices, each of which could carry satisfaction in their own way.

It is vital to be clear about what you want and what you want to feel and experience. It is also vital that you explore your reasons for taking particular actions. Be cautious of false promises from others and also not being completely honest with yourself about your motivations.

If there are too many choices, give watchful consideration to all of them and sleep on the bigger decisions before rushing in.

This can be a time of identity crisis, loss of self-confidence and possibly feeling undermined and inadequate.

It could also mean that you are indulging in wishful thinking and daydreaming and are lacking the necessary focus toward achieving your dreams and goals.

Eight of Cups

Keywords to Use

New path, walking away, no turning back, burning bridges.

Symbols

A Character Walking Away from the Cups

In other words, there is no looking back. The sun and moon are together, representing an eclipse.

Meaning

This can mean that you are in the process of walking away from an individual, situation or feeling. The individual might not be completely accepting their own feelings and emotions. The individual has obviously turned away from a certain path and is going in a different direction.

This is probably not an easy choice and the individual seems to realize that there may be complications on their path forward. The individual doesn't seem to want to take anything from the past with them, though there might be something that could help them.

This can also mean a profound discontent with a life that has been made on phony values and a longing to set off in search of something better or more meaningful.

The cups are all standing, and this indicates that the individual has attracted what they desire and then realized it was not truly what they wanted.

The Eight of Cups card can mean an emotional turning point which will lead to new arrangements. They should know that it is a time to move on to new things. This might be a physical change like moving, changing jobs or getting out of a relationship. It could also mean letting go of old beliefs and values.

Once this course of action has been started, there is really no turning back.

Nine of Cups

Keywords to Use

Joy, serenity, complacency, fulfilment.

Symbols

A Nobleman, Satisfied and Affluent

The cups are standing and in balance. This card is one of abundance and seeing your desires come true. It also shows pleasure when you get what you want.

Meaning

There is satisfaction, physical wellbeing, substantial achievement and looking forward to the future. The Nine of Cups is also about success, triumph and gratification.

It is a card of unadulterated indulgence. Enjoy it. You've truly earned it, and you have the right to savor every delightful feeling that comes with it.

However, do not let yourself to get too smug.

You can revel in your accomplishment, and you can celebrate life.

Ten of Cups

Keywords to Use

Domestic happiness, blessings, love, satisfaction, families.

Symbols

Cups in the Rainbow

There is a feeling of the fairy-tale-like dreams and happiness of being here on earth. The pair have extended arms, giving thanks for their blessings.

Meaning

With regard to goals, there will be accomplishment, success and celebration. The Ten of Cups is telling that life is the best it can be at this time.

There will be a brief break or a family vacation, and there will be a true sense of closeness and belonging.

There is happiness, love, wealth and satisfaction in all that you do. This peaceful scene may specify inner or outer peace. In addition, it could mean an end to a conflict.

Page of Cups

PAGE of CUPS.

Keywords to Use

Pregnancy, birth, the beginning of a new project, labor of love, inspiration, ideas.

Symbols

The Page

Represents a child, a person who is younger in age or more juvenile than the individual you are reading for.

As an individual, the Page is a delicate, imaginative child or an individual who has a childlike imagination. The child might be somewhat of a daydreamer, and is quiet, tender, thoughtful and kind.

Be careful of over-sensitivity.

Could be a child born under the signs of either Pisces, Cancer or Scorpio.

Meaning

The Page of Cups card shows news of a pregnancy or birth.

Be aware though that this can also mean the inspired birth of a new idea or project. Allow the ideas to flow freely in a creative manner. The ideas will be coming right you're your heart. It is vital not to judge these creative thoughts.

The Page may bring an opportunity for love, exploring your psychic nature, innate and spiritual matters. Proceed with an open mind and sense of interest and curiosity.

Knight of Cups

Keywords to Use

Delicate, idealistic, sensitive, affectionate, thoughtful, subtle.

Symbols

The Knight

Represents a young adult or an individual who is juvenile for their age. A dreamy, creative, complex, expressive and romantic individual.

Devoted, kind, generous and helpful, sometimes to their own disadvantage.

On the down side, this person can be too emotional and oversensitive and suffers from indifference.

This individual will often not want to hurt the feelings of others. Sometimes they are not able to say no when others ask for help.

This card might represent male or female, even though the character in the card appears to be a male.

The Knight of Cups card represents delightful moods and dreams, but the individual might struggle to motivate themselves or put their plans into action.

The Wings

Represent Mercury, the winged messenger. There may be someone bringing a message.

Meaning

Love, friendship and support.

If the Knight of Cups comes up in reading and there has formerly been a King or Queen of Cups car, it might be showing that the cards are still speaking about that earlier individual.

Queen of Cups

Keywords to Use

Sensitive, instinctive, kind, calm, creative, empathy, emotions.

Symbols

<u>Female</u>

She is a devoted, thoughtful, generous, nurturing, intuitive, sensitive, empathetic individual who is steered by her feelings and her heart.

She is the individual who others turn to with their issues and problems, which can be a challenge for her sometimes because she carries people's problems and worry for them.

Meaning

The Queen of Cups card is also about emotional contentment and connection to ourselves and our emotional state.

She has an imaginative, artistic side which may or may not be articulated. She can be very idealistic and occasionally have her head in the clouds.

This card is frequently considered to embody an individual who is born under the sign of Cancer, Pisces or Scorpio. Or, she may have a lot of those qualities in her character.

Approach any situation with tender, loving eyes of kindness and compassion. Always look for the highest good in the circumstances and the splendor in the individuals involved.

King of Cups

Keywords to Use

Loving, profound feelings, visionary, tender, imaginative.

Symbols

The Man

Most likely in his 40s or older.

He is mostly caring, loving, generous, calm, sensitive, very romantic and expressive.

He prefers to have peace and harmony everywhere around him. Because he does not like to upset others, it may lead to him not being honest with himself or those around him.

He can be somewhat of a fantasist and might not be the most driven individual to take action on his ideas. He is very imaginative but is a perfectionist.

On the adverse side, he sometimes suppresses his feelings and is withdrawn, critical, indecisive, has impracticable expectations and buries his head in the sand when there is an issue at hand.

Suit of Wands

Ace of Wands

Keywords to Use

New job, prospect or business, inspiration, accomplishment.

Symbols

<u>A Hand Emerging from a Cloud Holding a Wooden Stick</u>

New beginnings, inventiveness, achievement, invention, self-confidence, bravery, new things are offered or started. A symbol of possibility.

Meaning

The Ace of Wands card indicates a new job offer or business prospect. Or, it could be an opportunity in a current job like a promotion.

It could also mean a new project which will provide chances to use your creativity, expressiveness, growth, influence, inventiveness. Moving forward.

In business, it could mean new business prospects. It could also be an inspired project or hobby that somebody is working on. Or, it could also mean volunteer or charity work.

With the Ace of Wands, there is a lot of liveliness, inspiration, desire, accomplishment and moving forward. It is a card of beginnings.

It could also show personal growth and taking action in the direction of something you really want to do.

It is the time to act definitively and grip the prospects that are right in front of you. You definitely possess access to the resources you need. If not, those resources will open up as you move along. Don't fret. It is a time to take the initial step and set the wheels in motion.

Two of Wands

Keywords to Use

Individual power, strength, accomplishment, support, impatience.

Symbols

A Dapper, Well-off Man

He is surveying the scenery around him and is holding the world in his hand. One wand is secured to the wall and he is holding the other.

The Two of Wands is a card of accomplishment and success, of having reached a goal, and having the world in the palm of your hand. What's next?

Meaning

This can signify the success which you have earned, prosperity and wealth, all of which have been brought about by your efforts. Or, it could mean you will be receiving help and support from well-off people.

The Two of Wands is a card of individual power, strength, bravery and individual success. It is a card of power and it could mean that you have the power and impact that somebody else wants or somebody else has it and you want it. You might need to pursue the help of somebody in a place of influence, and that help will be open to you. It could also mean that somebody looks up to you and needs help opening doors for them.

It is also vital to ponder the impact that material power and achievement plays in your own life and goals. Are you motivated only by outward success?

There is some satisfaction for what has been accomplished and also searching for new prospects for inspiration or development.

There can be a certain amount of edginess and a longing to move onto new plans. The individual might be pondering new opportunities or even moving to a new place. There will be a choice between what is stable and moving onto new things.

Three of Wands

Keywords to Use

Lend, monetary support, goals, focus, direction.

Symbols

<u>A Man Facing the Sea with 3 Ships on the Water</u>

The man has 3 wands surrounding him which are supporting him. He is on a journey, doing his own thing and stopping to consider the goals in front of him.

Meaning

The Three of Wands card frequently appears when somebody has applied for a loan or a mortgage or is trying to get some sort of aid from somebody else in order to further their plans. This is a card of achievement.

The character is creating his own success and realizes that he must to take action it he wants something to happen. This is a card of courage.

There is positive support and cooperation from others with plans. There is a lot of thought and planning and plans may still be in the preparation stage, even though some action has been taken.

This is also a card of vision, seeing the big picture and taking a long-term view of matters. As the individual with the long-term view, you can guide and aid others to support yourself and also their best future.

This is also a card of leadership and being the first to enter into unexplored terrain, and others will follow you.

Be brave and move courageously into new areas. Once you set things into motion, undertaking your own thing and in your own way, you will be able to attract the resources and backing that you need.

Four of Wands

Keywords to Use

Wedding, partnership, festivity, achievement, household.

Symbols

Four Wands with Green Wreaths and Fruit

Indicates success and abundance.

Meaning

The Four of Wands is a card which regularly shows a marriage or engagement. It could also be a positive business partnership.

It can mean friends, partners or spouses entering into business together.

It means doing something creative as opposed to merely thinking about it. It could also be fruitful involvement in a club or hobby.

The Four of Wands is a card of celebration, success, stability, harmony, cooperation, agreement, permanency and accomplishment. Teamwork is on the horizon.

It can also show the 4 corners of the home and point towards successful conclusions of home projects.

Five of Wands

Keywords to Use

Fights, arguing, pettiness, disharmony, quarrels.

Symbols

People Battling with Wands

The closest one seems to be holding the others off with very little exertion.

Meaning

There are fights going on and tempers may be getting worn. There may be a lot of hostility directed at you. Nevertheless, by dealing calmly and peacefully with the issues, instead of offending the individuals concerned, you will find a good solution.

It is vital not to get into either office or family politics. If there are fights around you, you do not need to be involved or you can you just deal with what directly affects you.

The Five of Wands is a card of triviality, bickering and irritating disagreements.

You should create boundaries between yourself and the source of the squabbling. Distance yourself from what you can.

The Five of Wands is also a card of obstructions, aggravations, frustrations and things not going as you prefer them to. There is no agreement or cooperation with this card.

Six of Wands

Keywords to Use

Accomplishment, triumph, victory, admiration, acknowledgement.

Symbols

A Man Rides Holding a Wand

The wreath on the wand represents success.

Meaning

This is a card of achievement, praise, recognition, plans coming to a positive conclusion, affluence and earned triumph.

Enjoy the fruits of your labors. The rewards you receive are well deserved.

This is not necessarily a card of being dominant over somebody else. It is more about the conquest over yourself and your environment.

It is also significant to have a healthy self-esteem and permit yourself to feel good about your accomplishments, without acting as if you are greater than others.

Seven of Wands

Keywords to Use

Fights, unfair numbers, in control, on top of the situation.

Symbols

A Man Holding a Wand Battling With 6 Other Wands

He is on top of the situation and is fighting from a solid vantage point.

The man is wearing a shoe and a boot. The foot with the boot is in water, which indicates mastery over emotions.

Meaning

The Seven of Wands is a card of continuing fighting. It might be a cautioning not to get involved with fighting other people's battles lest it is truly required.

This can mean that somebody is attacking you (though it may not be physically). It can be you going to battle with others. There are power struggles present and someone else may be trying to gain control over you. You must you're your courage in the face of adversity.

This can also mean an unfair fight if you are dealing with more than one individual or problem at the same time.

It could be something that you have to fight on your own. It may be telling you to get some backup. The Seven of Wands is a card of self-defense and it might be essential to protect your space or ground. Maybe you need to create boundaries and stand up for yourself.

You might need to secure your position and stand up for what is right and what you believe in. This is a card of hostility and rebelliousness.

Eight of Wands

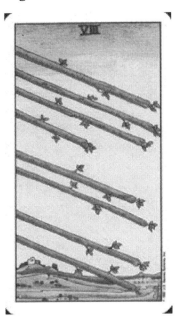

Keywords to Use

Travel, abroad, speediness, movement, action.

Symbols

Eight Wands Moving Through the Air Over Water

This shows things are happening rapidly and often means travel.

This could mean arriving quickly at your goal or destination.

Meaning

The Eight of Wands is a card of movement. It is the best time to take action and move onward speedily with a plan. Things are moving very fast around you.

This shows something you have been waiting for coming to an end. Therefore, the time is right for change. It is a card of fulfilment and accomplishment and circumstances moving forward.

Maybe you have dreaming about an idea. Now is a good time to take action because things will move speedily for you.

This can also be a decent time to rejoice in the successes of a past project and then move onto something new.

Nine of Wands

Keywords to Use

Fighting, strength of will, resolve, triumph.

Symbols

A Battle–Scarred Man in Front of 8 Wands Clutching the 9th

His battle is behind him, though it has not been without individual cost and likely wounds.

The 8 wands are secure in the ground as if forming a barrier between him and his problems.

Meaning

While he appears to be in control at the moment, he has an appearance of carefulness and doubt on his face. He is prepared to take on trouble, wherever it might be coming from.

He appears to be expecting more misfortune, and he is ready to attack it when it comes. Be alert and prepared.

Even if you are feeling injured and reaching the end of your rope, you are still prepared to fight on. You might want to draw on all your reserves in order to carry on as the battling might not be over.

Pause, regroup yourself, and give yourself a pat on the back for the conquests you have won and how far you have come.

Prepare yourself for the ensuing round, because whatever it is you are facing is not completely over, though you are much closer to the finish line than you might think.

Ten of Wands

Keywords to Use

Overwhelm, overextend, problems, test.

Symbols

The Man is Carrying 10 Wands

He has his head suppressed in the wands so he can't see where he is going nor can he see how near he is to his journey's end.

Meaning

The Ten of Wands is a card of being overwhelmed, oppression, being over-burdened with responsibilities and work. The man looks as though he has taken on much more than he can carry and is carrying the wands in a very ineffective way.

You might also be feeling troubled because you have taken on the difficulties and possibly the workload of other individuals.

The man runs the risk of dropping the whole lot. He has his head buried and can't see where he is going because he has taken on too much. It might be that the individual feels that they must carry this heavy load by themselves. It could also mean that they need to get help from others.

It is not helpful to wait for others to notice that you need help and offer it to you. You may be waiting a long time.

The Ten of Wands is a card of struggle and doing things the tough way. You might have to take accountability for something or not take the blame for something.

Do your best to lighten your load as much as you can by not taking on any more and practice saying no.

Page of Wands

Keywords to Use

Communication, news, fiery child, high energy.

Meaning

Individuals characterized by the Page of Wands can be children born under the signs of Aries, Leo or Sagittarius. They can also be individuals who are younger and less matured than the person being read.

They are rather fiery, outgoing, artistic individuals with a bright temperament. They can be child-like and juvenile and have an immense focus on themselves.

They are also to be expected to be high energy, eager free spirits. They can be impulsive, fidgety and not finish what they've started.

Situation

The Page of Wands is a card that regularly carries news of some type. This can be new beginnings and prospects for you to be imaginative and passionate.

The news that The Page conveys will frequently entail you to take action fairly swiftly.

This may be a prospect that stimulates you and maybe reawakens your child-like sense of wonder, curiosity, desire and eagerness.

Professional ventures denoted by this card can be risky and not well thought out.

Knight of Wands

Keywords to Use

Property, transfer, new property, act, hurry.

Meaning

The Knight of Wands represents is a very high energy individual who lives their life in the fast lane and has a habit of doing everything at fast speed.

This can be an impulsive, reckless individual who is susceptible to abrupt changes and does not finish what they start.

They are exciting, self-confident, outgoing and enjoyable to be around but might not be very reliable because they are off onto their next project.

They can be very passionate and hot tempered. The Knight of Wands individual has a enormous heart and is very generous but may also be insensitive.

Situation

The Knight of Wands repeatedly shows up relative to property. This may be a move of either a home or office or it can be purchasing an additional property.

There is regularly a sense of urgency and things happening hurriedly with the Knight of Wands card.

Queen of Wands

Keywords to Use

Professional female, achievement, leadership, resourceful.

Meaning

The Queen of Wands is a card that typically represents a woman of any age. She appears to be an independent, strong-willed business professional.

She is a natural-born leader and will often be in a position of leadership or owns a business.

If she does not own a business, she is more than capable of doing so. As an individual, she is eager, passionate, a great thinker, generous, action oriented, active, reliable, skilled, practical, self-confident, a good organizer, imaginative and forward thinking.

She is popular, outgoing, tackles everything enthusiastically, is open and genuine, has a natural vitality, is self-assured and happy.

On the negative side, she can be overbearing, domineering, controlling, intolerant and lacking in the area of tact. She may have trouble delegating and believes that nobody else is as capable of doing things as she is.

Situation

This is a perfect time to take a look at your own resources and maybe work on your own self-development. There may be academic opportunities surrounding you at the moment.

Kings of Wands

Keywords to Use

Leader, professional, accomplishment, risk taker, hard worker.

Meaning

The King of Wands is a card that has many of the same characteristics as the Queen. He is a high energy, a go-getter, action oriented, strongminded, inspirational, forceful man who knows what he wants and how to get there. He produces results and is very content to bask in the glory of his success.

He is a brave, devoted man and will regularly be in business or at the very least a position of leadership.

He is not afraid to take risks. He is a mature man who will think through the risks and rewards and then take action. If things don't work out, he will evaluate the circumstances, learn from them and then move on.

He can have a fiery temper and always says what he thinks. Like the Queen, tact is not his strong point. When he has said what needs to be said, it is over and finished. He is not an individual who holds grudges.

He may be overbearing from time to time, but his heart is in the right place and he does mean well.

Situation

This card can be asking you to take action in a daring and courageous way.

Suit of Swords

Ace of Swords

Keywords to Use

Thoughts, beginnings, victory, resolve, focus.

Symbols

A Hand Holding a Sword with a Crown on Top and the Wreath of Success in the Crown

This is a card of beginnings, as with all the Aces. But beware as it can be a double-edged sword.

Meaning

The Ace of Swords is a card which represents a new beginning, new ideas, a renewed (or new) strength of will and mental energy. This is a card of triumph and achievement.

The Ace of Swords frequently indicates new focus and improved clarity surrounding an important decision. It is a sign that you have the strength and power within yourself to achieve whatever needs to be done.

The opportunities presented by the Ace of Swords are expected to be challenging and you'll most likely have to call on the full might of your will or personality in order to attain your goals. However, the crown at the top of the sword shows that you will be successful if you do so.

It specifies the need for bravery, creativity and willpower. It also calls for a truthful and moral approach. There is often a strong sense of understanding of what needs to be done and an aptitude to cut through immaterial things.

The Ace of Swords can also speak of truth and justice - to defending a cause and standing up for what you believe is right.

Two of Swords

Keywords to Use

Indecisiveness, absence of clarity, misunderstanding, concern, anxiety.

Meaning

The individual doesn't know what to do and doesn't seem to be able to see all the needed info and cannot think clearly. She/he might be struggling to see the consequences of their actions.

The Two of Swords is a card of indecisiveness. It can also be a card of recognizing that something must be done about a specific situation and being in denial.

You have a tough choice or decision to make. It is a decision you perhaps need to make logically. There is a lot of emotion involved in this choice or decision (symbolized by the water).

The choice could be one that is producing a great deal of anxiety and concern. If there are other individuals involved, then the choice may hurt or upset someone. You have to do what is best for you.

The crossed swords mean that the individual has created a huge barrier. It is almost as if you are trying to block your emotions and push everybody out.

You may be reluctant to accept the truth about a situation or feelings and try to deny the existence of same.

Three of Swords

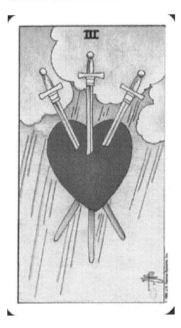

Keywords to Use

Arguments, heartache, grief, struggle

Symbols

Three swords piercing a heart. This is the only one of the Swords Cards that does not have an individual in it.

Meaning

The Three of Swords is a card of heartbreak. It could be an argument, it could literally be a heart attack, or it could be a miscarriage in a pregnancy (which will depend upon the cards with surround it).

There are expected to be some raw emotions with the circumstances surrounding this card, though they may or may not be voiced.

There is sadness, grief, conflict, struggle, distress and much emotional pain.

If it is a disagreement, it might be that there are things that must be said in order to clear things up, as painful as that be.

Four of Swords

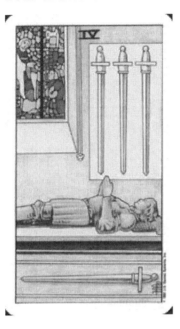

Keywords to Use

Recovery, retreat, unwind, destress, seclusion, time out.

Meaning

The Four of Swords is a card of relaxation, healing, recuperation, retreat and solitude and shows a physical and mental need to take some time out and just simply do nothing.

This might be a time of silent contemplation and preparation for your next steps in life. It is also a good time for your mind, body and spirit to heal.

The Four of Swords will frequently appear for somebody who is overworked, stressed and worn out.

It can also appear for somebody who is recuperating from a sickness, and it is vital for them to permit themselves to mend fully prior to starting to do too much again.

Five of Swords

Keywords to Use

Conflict, triumph, strong opponent, hollow win.

Meaning

The Five of Swords is a card of battle and triumph, but at the expense of other individuals. The man on the card looks rather arrogant with possessing all of the swords. However, this can be a hollow conquest. This might also be a serious disagreement.

Maybe you are up against somebody who is much tougher than you are and they have all the cards in their favor. However, it might be you that is stronger.

The Five of Swords is a card of arguments and aggression, and it might be an "us-against-them" approach. This card is one of selfishness and no cooperation between people.

There are no real winners. One individual possesses all of the swords, often to the disadvantage of the other parties.

Six of Swords

Keywords to Use

Improved conditions, look past present pain, move ahead

Symbols

A Man Rowing a Boat with Two Passengers

They are rowing out of the choppy waters and into the calmer seas ahead. The 6 swords are in front of them in the boat, suggesting that they might be taking their worries with them. The swords do not impale the boat in any way, so the effect of past contention could be much less now.

Meaning

This Six of Swords is a card which indicates that things are improving and you are heading into better conditions. On this matter, use your head over your heart and go with the logic of a situation.

You are most likely moving away from stress, worry, hurt and struggle and into improved circumstances, though it can from time to time be tough to see beyond the pain and to concentrate on the good.

This Six of Swords is also a card of physical journeys as well as the journey of self-development and change.

Do yourself a favor and let go of the pain of the past and allow yourself to move forward into a better place, particularly spiritually and mentally.

Seven of Swords

Keywords to Use

Theft, loss, sneaking away, deceitful, sneaky, sly.

Meaning

The Seven of Swords is a card which represents something being taken away, usually in a very underhanded, sneaky fashion.

It is a card of craftiness and cunning, hinting to remove yourself from a situation. It could mean that somebody is attempting to sneak out of a situation, rather than to confront the person and deal with the matter amenably.

The look on the man's face appears as though he believes he has got away with something which he is aware that he really should not have done.

Notice that he is carrying the swords in a very inept way and is not watching where he is going. Therefore, those swords could easily slip onto his feet.

It is probable that he will get caught, or at the very least his actions will come back to bite him. This can be a thief, a spy, a liar or a person who is committing some kind of fraud or wrong doing.

If somebody is considering actions which are not legal or ethical, the Seven of Swords can be a warning that they will get caught. If they do, it is most likely due to their own feelings of guilt.

Eight of Swords

Keywords to Use

Restriction, boundaries, hindrances, stuck.

Symbols

Blindfolded Woman with Cloths Tied Around Her

Movement is restricted.

She is Standing in Water

This represents emotions.

Meaning

The Eight of Swords is a card of restriction. It may be self-inflicted and the circumstances might not be as problematic as they are perceived to be. Restriction and obstacles from external and internal sources.

The clothes seem to be very loose around the woman, and she could probably wiggle loose and remove the blindfold if she wanted to.

The Eight of Swords can be a card of limiting beliefs about your abilities. Sometimes it is also a card of "I just can't because…" which might or might not be justified.

You or someone you know may have a feeling of being stuck, backed into a corner or restrained by somebody or by your surroundings.

This could mean that somebody has given away their own power to somebody else. It could be that you are feeling like a victim in life and are waiting for somebody or something to rescue you.

Some of this situation might be of your own doing. However, you still have choices, as hard as that might seem to admit. By finding your clarity of thought, you will discover an answer and a way to move forward.

Nine of Swords

Keywords to Use

Heartache, anguish, pain, despair, sickness, stress.

Meaning

The Nine of Swords is a card indicating grief, desolation, hopelessness, great hurt, worry, anxiety and sorrow. It might also show health problems and hospital visits.

This will indicate some sort of stress-related condition. With regard to women, the Nine of Swords can indicate women's health issues or sometimes even surgery.

The head in the hands indicates a refusal to look at the world or burying your head in the sand in the hope that your problems will disappear.

Late at night is the time when all your uncertainties, worries, doubts, feelings of guiltiness and anxiety come to the surface. At times, the pain of these feelings is so much that we just put our head in our hands and cry.

This might mean that you must take a step back and observe the choices you are making in life. Maybe a slight change could make a vast difference in the way you feel and the actions you take moving forward.

Ten of Swords

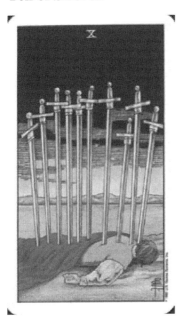

Keywords to Use

Beginnings and endings, disappointed, let down, unease, stabbed in the back.

Symbols

A Man with 10 Swords Pierced into His Back

The Ten of Swords is a card of feeling like you have been let down/stabbed in the back by somebody. It is also a card of worry, loss and bad luck.

Meaning

Similar to the Death card in representation, the Ten of Swords indicates that something has come to end.

Symbolically, the situation is dead. However, there is probably also some sort of rebirth and renewal.

This card represents a new day dawning. Your darkest hour is just before dawn. Your pain or loss will not be minimized, but it is a sign that there is hope in the future.

Over-reaction, making a mountain out of a molehill, hypochondriac or a drama queen are all good examples of someone associated with this card.

Page of Swords

PAGE of SWORDS

Keywords to Use

Childlike, erratic, impulsive, antagonistic, defensive.

Meaning

This can be a person who is very quick-witted and sharp tongued. They can be a bit of a gossiper and a trouble- maker.

He/she is likely to be juvenile and perhaps inclined to have temper tantrums to get their own way.

There is little to no compassion with this individual. They are impatient, critical, cynical and have no real understanding of the effect of their words on the feelings of other individuals.

It can be a child who is bright and lively, with a quick mind and vivid imagination.

The Page of Swords sometimes describes things being done in too much of a hurry, with little thought to the consequences. There is intolerance, recklessness and not much caring about the involvement of other individuals.

Knight of Swords

Keywords to Use

Rush, risk-taker, absence of thought, haste, thoughtless, reckless.

Meaning

The Knight of Swords is a card that symbolizes somebody who is rushing hurried into something without giving it any real thought.

The individual is impulsive, headstrong and full of eccentric ideas. They are talented and unafraid and can be an impulsive risk-taker.

They can be a good communicator, but they can also be insensitive, cynical, blunt and bad-mannered. This individual can be someone who is quite immature and convinced of their own superiority.

If you are friends, this person is a strong ally and fight in your corner. But they can be inconsistent and quirky and you should be careful placing long-term trust in them.

This card can indicate unexpected events, where somebody must take charge swiftly so that the whole thing does not result in total pandemonium. If you are considering delegating a project, be cautious of the individual you choose to take on that important role.

Queen of Swords

Keywords to Use

Tough, independent, widow, truthful, perceptive, straight-forward.

Symbols

The Queen

Can show as male or female, although will mostly show up as a female. This card often represents an elder individual, possibly somebody who is widowed or on their own.

Meaning

As an individual, this person is very straightforward and likely has a sharp tongue and can be mocking and harsh.

This person is quick-witted, smart, rational, critical, can be discerning and does not take to fools very well. He/she can be very insightful and see through individuals and situations rather fast.

He/she is authentic, truthful and may take the moral high ground with others. This person is not one to be messed with or lied to. She is tough and independent and likely to keep her feelings to herself until she blows.

This person likes to be in control. They can be soft on the inside but works very hard to make sure they do not let others see that they might be vulnerable at times.

The Queen of Swords is a card which can indicate hard bargains and negotiating. The matter is expected to be dealt with by following the rule book. There will be little to no room for emotions.

King of Swords

Keywords to Use

Entrepreneur, truthful, competent, detail, common-sense, analytical.

Meaning

The King of Swords often shows up as a man of law, maybe a lawyer or policeman.

As a businessman, he is forthright, tough, usually fair and truthful in his connections.

He will not take nonsense from anyone and has a very clear idea of where he is headed in life. He is smart, quick-witted, detail-oriented, logical and resourceful.

He typically takes an unemotional approach to matters. He can be firm, stern and inflexible when it comes to sticking to the rules.

In matters of the heart, he can be cut off from his feelings, which can appear as cynicism, mockery and severe independence.

The King of Swords is telling you that you need a balanced, rational, systematic approach where hopes should be realistic.

In other words, you should think with your head and not your heart.

Suit of Pentacles

Ace of Pentacles

Keywords to Use

New source of money, monetary prospect, steady money flow.

Symbols

A Hand Holding a Coin

Suggests plenty.

Meaning

The Ace of Pentacles, as with all the Aces, symbolizes a beginning and something new being presented.

This will frequently be a new source of finances arriving for somebody. It is typically additional money being provided from somewhere you usually receive funds, maybe a raise at your employment.

It basically means new opportunities leading to increased success. The Ace of Pentacles shows a change for the better monetarily, or the opportunities are there for you to improve your financial state of affairs.

You will perhaps have to take some action of your own in order to benefit from this new flow of money. It can also mean better money management.

Two of Pentacles

Keywords to Use

Juggling finances and life in general, going around in circles, busyness

Meaning

The Two of Pentacles is a card of juggling, mostly with finances. It is about going around in fruitless circles and not getting much done on a practical level.

There are continuous variations with money and you may need to budget better.

There might be so much going on that the individual is merely staying afloat with everything.

There is a denial as to much hot water they may be in or could be in down the road.

The Two of Pentacles calls for flexibility and variability. It is simply not the time to be immovable or unyielding in anything. It might always be showing you that you need to give something to someone else to handle.

The number 2 represents balance or lack thereof, choices and duality.

Interestingly, the pentacles are linked through a figure 8, the sign of infinity. This is joining both sides of the brain and brings reason and emotion together.

It might telling you that you need to focus on one thing at a time and do that one thing well.

Three of Pentacles

Keywords to Use

Education, new skills, learning, apprentice, professional, foundations.

Symbols

Craftsman Doing Work on a Pillar

This individual is an acknowledged expert which has come about through both learning and experience.

Meaning

The Three of Pentacles is a card of learning, studying and developing a talent which is useful in the workplace.

This can mean the individual is a student learning his/her craft or trade. This card will often come up for somebody when they are beginning a course of study. It could be for pleasure or a work-related skill. It is a card of accomplishment through applying oneself and become skilled at the subject.

This card can also indicate training and lessons being learned in life circumstances from somebody who is more knowledgeable in that subject than you. It is applied learning which may go together with theoretic learning.

With this card, there is regularly a need for cooperation from a third party, typically somebody whose know-how is required or assistance from a professional. It is a card of cooperation and collaboration to get a job done successfully. The laying of foundations is important to get things right at this point.

Four of Pentacles

Keywords to Use

Save your money, budget, trapped, lack of movement

Meaning

The Four of Pentacles appears to be trying hard to hold onto the little cash and physical belongings he has. This indicates the need to be extremely cautious with your spending at the moment and to avoid needless overindulgence. Perhaps you should create a better budget.

However, it might also indicate somebody who is being very stingy with their money and hanging on to every penny they have. It all depends upon the cards surrounding it.

That being the case, their money could be a source of tension and worry to them because they live in fear of losing it or never having enough. Money is not a source of happiness to this person, and may cause strife.

While somebody is determinedly holding onto what they have, there is no room for everything to flow and there is also no room for anything to flow in. The Four of Pentacles is a card of obstructions surrounding. It can also signify a person who is preoccupied with hoarding material wealth.

This is a card of trying to control and uphold the status quo.

Five of Pentacles

Keywords to Use

Absence, economic hardship, struggle, desperate, spiritual deficiency.

Symbols

The 5 Pentacles and 2 Desolate People

They have no way to become part of the world around them or even be aware of its existence.

Meaning

The Five of Pentacles symbolizes financial absence or loss, conflict, debt, worry and all the problems that come about from a severe lack of money. This is a card of financial trouble. There is also a feeling of hopelessness.

This card can also show money that is tied up or perhaps lost in a financial dealing.

It can also specify that somebody isn't going to receive as much money as they were expecting.

It might also indicate spiritual deficiency and a sense that life is worthless and that there is nobody to turn to for help and leadership.

The absence and neglect might also be associated with health and not taking care of ourselves appropriately.

Whether the destitution is over finances, wellbeing, emotional or spiritual matters, it is vital to realize that it will pass. Action must be taken in order to move forward.

Six of Pentacles

Keywords to Use

Abundantly, plenty, charity, monetary help, charitable

Symbols

A Wealthy Man Giving Money to Those in Need

He is wisely balancing out what he is giving, to be fair to all (which represents the scales of justice in his hand).

Meaning

The Six of Pentacles is a card of abundance. The gentleman has extra money to give to charity and help others. He is caring and generous.

There is spare money surrounding you.

This can be a card of balancing the books, or paying back money that is owed or being paid money back from somebody.

There may also be financial assistance on the way from somebody who is in a situation to offer help.

This might be in the form of a loan or gift or possibly a grant.

You may be a supporter to somebody else. With the Six of Pentacles, you could be the giver or the receiver.

Seven of Pentacles

Keywords to Use

Fruits of your labor, earned accomplishment, keep on moving forward, assessment

Symbols

Man, in Garden with 7 Pentacles

Pausing to look at what he has created.

Meaning

Money will be arriving soon from projects you have in the works. You have come a long way with a project and while you are able to pause and take a look at what you have accomplished and created, it is vital to keep going and finish it as rewards are on the way.

In addition, the Seven of Pentacles can appear for somebody who has put in a lot of effort, perhaps for free, and is at the point of giving up since they are not seeing the rewards coming fast enough.

It is imperative to recognize the progress that has been achieved thus far. It is a time of reflection to be sure that you are heading in the direction of your dreams.

The Seven of Pentacles can show up where somebody is at a crossroads with the choice to make as to whether they stay with what they are doing or move on to something else. It is a time of assessment and perhaps wanting to do something somewhat different in order to earn the rewards that are due.

Sometimes the toughest part is the final bit as you can see the project is mostly finished. However, it is frequently the last little bit of exertion that will finish the project and bring in the financial return.

This can specify rewards from earlier investments which have been wisely thought out.

The money that will come yours and is well deserved.

Eight of Pentacles

Keywords to Use

Career gratification, creation money, imagination, growth

Symbols

A Man Working with Eight Pentacles

He is literally "making money". Six are finished and hanging up. The man is working on one, and there is another one waiting to be completed.

Meaning

The Eight of Pentacles is a card about working at something that you love and making money for doing it. There is creativity, fulfilment, a certain amount of talent and mental stimulus in the work you do.

This can be somebody who is making a hobby or a passion into a business and receiving money from it or becoming self-employed.

It could also mean somebody works with their hands and is enjoying the work that they do.

The Eight of Pentacles is a card of the craftsman. It sometimes means perfecting skills you have or learning new skills.

This individual has a sense of pride and of a job well done. It is a card of applying yourself completely and meticulously to what you are doing and you will gain the rewards from it, in every sense of the word.

Nine of Pentacles

Keywords to Use

Wealth, stability, safety, affluence, self-reliance

Symbols

A Wealthy Woman with Pentacles All Around

Havin no worries from a financial point-of-view.

Meaning

The Nine of Pentacles is a card which means financial stability and security. It means more than simply income coming from your employment. Your income and wealth may be coming from real estate, savings accounts and other investments. This can also be "unexpected or unearned" income.

There is a sense of seclusion when the Nine of Pentacles shows up, though the lady seems pretty contented with that. An individual might be on their own, but there look as if there is financial provision for them, either of their own making or from somebody else.

The Nine of Pentacles could be a female or male of leisure who doesn't really need to work. It could also signify an entrepreneur or "self-made" business person who has worked hard in the past for their financial stability and they can afford to take time off and to enjoy the fruits of their labor.

This card may also show somebody who has expensive taste and can be extravagant. This is more than likely an individual who chooses quality over quantity and selects the best items they can afford.

Ten of Pentacles

Keywords to Use

Wealth, inheritance, family money

Symbols

3 Generations with Pentacles Surrounding Them

There is affluence, luxury, stability, wealth, material security and extravagance.

Meaning

The Ten of Pentacles is a card which frequently specifies that a sum of money is heading your way. It might be family money or an inheritance of some kind or money that is yours in some other way.

It sometimes also indicates a sum of money from which has come, or will come, your way, expected or unexpected.

It could also show generosity and monetary funding from a family member or sponsor.

This may also indicate success from a business. This card is about customs and agreements and can show a need to make financial/business preparations that will work in the long-term future.

Page of Pentacles

PAGE of PENTACLES

Keywords to Use

Hands-on, business ideas, creativity, enjoyment, ability to attract resources

Meaning

This might be a kid or an individual who is considerably younger than the person being read. It might be a pupil who does not find studying to be easy but who attains success by persevering.

This person is trustworthy, loyal, dependable, hard-working, logical, well-organized and likes to see material success.

On the negative side, this person is more than likely detached, a slave-driver (of themselves and others), stubborn, stiff, stubborn and craves acknowledgement. They absolutely do not like change or things which upset their routine. They need to have discipline in their life and a routine to work with.

With the Page of Pentacles, you never really need to worry about money. It will always be there for you when you need it, even if it is sometimes a little out of reach.

This card can lead you to studies that will involve attention to detail. It can appear for somebody who is in a rut with their job and needs to make a change.

Knight of Pentacles

Keywords to Use

Immovable, stubborn, best of everything, persistent, careful, practical, hard worker, hates change

Meaning

This can be a male or a female. This person is practical, predictable, easy-going, hardworking, strong-minded, persistent, detail-oriented, meticulous, detailed, judicious, vigilant, saves money and enjoys the comfort of financial security. They place great value on material comforts and insist on having the best of everything.

On the negative side, this person might be lacking in humor and is very unemotional.

They can be persistent, stiff, stubborn, lacking ambition and severely resistant to change. Do not change the status quo of this person's life or they will be very angry.

They can be perfectionists an obsessive about it. They might also work so hard to afford the material comforts that they tend to forget to factor in any time to enjoy the things they have worked so hard to achieve.

The Knight of Pentacles is a card which indicates an impasse or things not moving as fast as you would like. It might be that once the results come, they will be worth the exertion. There could also be a need to push the situation along a bit rather than just banging your head against a wall. You need to move on.

Queen of Pentacles

Keywords to Use

Hands-on, business-like, organized, stability, connection with earth and nature.

Meaning

The Queen of Pentacles is organized, matter-of-fact, hands-on, down-to–earth, and she appreciates candid connections with others. She is authentic and dependable, generous, action and detail-oriented, great at balancing the budget and juggling home and family life. She is smart and practical.

She enjoys surrounding herself with decent quality things and will typically purchase the best that she can pay for. She is largely a great manager of money and loves to have the security of money around her.

She might be an entrepreneur. She might also be the kind of individual who makes an outstanding behind-the-scenes organizer. She does not really desire fame and regularly wishes to support somebody else in their desire instead.

She is devoted, caring, generous, nurturing, and might have a love of nature and/or gardening. She loves to nurture and care for others, providing much support to them. She is frequently the individual who has a household full of strays and waifs, animals and plants. She will always provide a warm welcome to everyone.

The Queen of Pentacles is pointing in the direction of stability in your life. This is both emotional and financial. Youi will have an intimacy with the earth and nature and all things real.

King of Pentacles

Keywords to Use

Business individual, money, monetary transactions, carefulness, check things wisely.

Symbols

A Well-Dressed King Sitting on His Thrown

He appears to be more thoughtful about money than his surroundings.

He has a hard interior and is shielding himself from everything emotional.

Meaning

As an individual, this can be male or female. They are more than likely an entrepreneur or somebody involved with money. They are pleasant and influential when you meet them.

The Kind of Pentacles type of person is shrewd and sharp with the ability to win with negotiation. Their first priority in any deal will be themselves, specifically how they are going to benefit financially.

You might notice that they charmingly and gracefully promise you one thing orally, and then the written contract might not quite coincide with what they promised. This person likes to be in control of all circumstances concerning money.

Be very cautious with this individual, mainly in professional and financial transactions. Check everything cautiously and be sure that you recognize precisely where you stand prior to committing yourself to anything with them.

Be cautious of the individual handling the money in business, official and monetary transactions.

Tarot Card Spreads

The Celtic Cross Spread

The Celtic Cross Spread is very powerful, because it can show the overall result of a situation but only if you don't make any changes. It will also indicate your hopes about a specific situation, your deepest fears and the impact of the individuals surrounding you with regard to the situation and your choices.

This is one of the most popular spreads and is used most often. You can use it for the telling of a general overview of a specific situation. It can also be used for asking particular questions, mainly if you are searching for alternative results, asking questions like - "What would be the result if I did this or that?"

It is imperative to remember that the result is grounded upon the individual's present state of mind and feelings and assumes that the individual is going to do nothing to change that outcome.

However, The Celtic Cross Spread can also be useful to compare outcomes if specific actions are taken. This is frequently called the "Alternate Future". For instance, "What will be the outcome if I choose to remain in my current job?" and "What will be the outcome if I choose to take a new job that I have been presented with?"

The Celtic Cross Spread should be used as a basic starting spread to highlight explicit subjects for more examination. It can then be used very successfully to discover those questions.

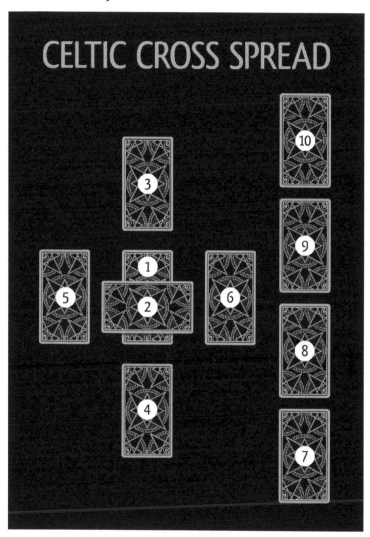

Position 1

The situation.

Position 2

Lays across Position 1 as shown and will often bring up the actual problem or challenge. This is the opposing factor.

Position 3

Above Positions 1 and 2 and includes added detail to the current situation. Consider this the root cause of the problem.

Position 4

Placed below Cards 1 and 2, it indicates the past.

Position 5

Placed left or right of the cross, it specifies influences in the past. It can also sometimes be the goal of the person being read. (the left or right position will depend which direction the significator is looking).

Position 6

Placed to the left or right of the cross, it shows the close future. (the left or right position will depend which direction the significator is looking).

Position 7

Placed at the bottom of the vertical line, it indicates the fears of the person being read. This can also mean how you see yourself.

Position 8

Placed right above Card 7, it indicates other individuals. It might signify matters of the household.

Position 9

Placed directly above Card 8, it indicates the hopes and desires of the person being read. There is regularly significant direction with this card.

Position 10

Placed at the top of the row, it shows the outcome.

For more info, you can build another row from bottom to top alongside the first one. You can keep accumulating rows, which will give you even more info.

You would only generally do this if the outcome is not clear. This may be that the inquiry is unclear or has not yet been decided.

When you add further rows to the Celtic Cross Spread, it will add significantly further awareness to the reading.

You can read up the columns from bottom to top. You can also read diagonally across each line, so you have added info on fears, the impact of other individuals, hopes and the outcome.

The 21 Card Romany Spread

The 21 Card Romany Spread is also very useful. It involves 21 cards which are laid out in 3 rows of 7 cards. These cards signify the ast, the present and the future.

This spread is perfect for practicing reading cards that fall next to each other in a sequence. The cards in the 21 Card Romany Spread proceed to tell a story from beginning to end. This is a spread that would be great to use when practicing your skills of reading tarot cards.

There are no definite positions for this spread. However, it can be extremely beneficial as an overall outline of the read, and you can then explore in further detail questions that may come up. This spread also provides a good suggestion of individuals that may be involved in the situation.

This spread is customarily just called the Romany Spread, and it is a very easy spread to learn in order to get an awareness of what happened in the past. This is what is having an effect on the "querant's" (person asking the question or person you are reading for) life now and the overall way things are developing in the present and how they are most likely going to unfold moving ahead into the future. That is - if no changes are made.

The Romany Spread contains 3 rows of 7 cards, laid out from right to left, starting at the bottom of the table (closest to you, the reader).

First - lay out 7 cards - this is the past. Next, lay out another row of 7 cards - this is the present.

Finally, lay out an additional row of 7 cards - this is the future result.

From there, proceed on to read from card 1, from right to left, and build up the story of what is happening as you go along from card to card.

Know that, if needed, you can lay out added rows after that if you want or need to get more info going on the developments of the circumstances. Each added row provides further info. This could be info moving forward into the future or it may be adding further to the entire situation.

*See below a construction of what the spread looks like:

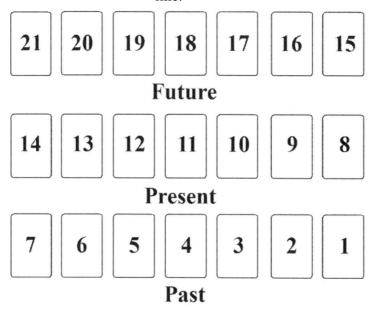

| 21 | 20 | 19 | 18 | 17 | 16 | 15 |

Future

| 14 | 13 | 12 | 11 | 10 | 9 | 8 |

Present

| 7 | 6 | 5 | 4 | 3 | 2 | 1 |

Past

The Astrology Spread

The Astrology Spread is very easy to use. Below this explanation is an image of the spread for you to refer to. You will put 1 card in each of the positions around the circle. This gives you an indication of the following 12 months. The first month will be the current month. If you are very close to the end of the month, month 1 can be started on the following month.

Then, place a card in the center of the circle. This card will set the tone for the whole year.

Proceed to go around again, adding a new card to each of the months. Because you have 78 cards in a tarot deck, you are able to go around 6 whole times, using 72 of the cards.

You are also able to add a 13th card to the one in the center of the circle with each additional round of cards if you desire. If you choose to do it this way, you will end up using all of the cards in the deck.

There will be 6 cards for each month, and that will provide you with quite a bit of info.

Place your cards side by side, proceeding outwards from each individual card, as you go around every time, and that way you will end up with 6 cards beside each other for every month. You can read each month from right to left proceeding outwards.

You are allowed to go around the circle as few or as many times as you want, or need. It is completely up to you, and you should know that there is no right or wrong way. You should use as many cards as you feel comfortable with.

The Astrology Spread is good if an individual wants a general overview of their life. After that, you can use other spreads for added detail in specific areas or to ask more thorough questions about certain areas of life.

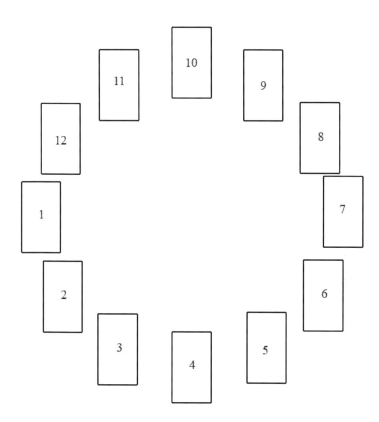

The Astrology Spread can also be used to denote the 12 houses of an individual's life in astrology. This is beneficial to gain additional info into a specific area. And again, you can add more cards to each house for more detail.

The 12 houses in astrology are as follows:

1) **Aries** - personality, situation, how others see the person being read, self.

2) **Taurus** - money, belongings, earning power and monetary values.

3) **Gemini** - travel and communication, day-to-day events.

4) **Cancer** - homelife, siblings, family, parents.

5) **Leo** - pleasure, passion, love affairs, vacations, self-expression, creativity.

6) **Virgo** - work and health – both emotional and physical.

7) **Libra** – partnerships – personal and professional - and marriage, legal situations.

8) **Scorpio** - inherit, decease, sex, other people's money, endings and beginnings.

9) **Sagittarius** - philosophy, education, visions, travel and long-distance trips.

10) **Capricorn** - occupation, career, recognition, reputation.

11) **Aquarius** - friends, organizations, hopes and desires.

12) **Pisces** - problems, limitations, undisclosed fears, adversaries, dangers, subconscious.

As you are going around the spread, if you get any of the Major Arcana Cards, they denote significant influences in your life. These influences might be people or beliefs or character traits which are impacting you in a positive or challenging way. The Major Arcana Cards could also mean certain noteworthy events or situations.

When doing the Astrology Spread, if you draw a lot of people cards from the Major Arcana or from the Court Cards of the Minor Arcana, they might be certain personalities or individuals who are having a great effect on your life. This will be either in that month (if you are doing a 12-month spread) or in that area of life (if you are using the Astrology Houses).

If the personalities of the individuals do not mean anything to you, or you cannot relate to those individuals, then the Court Cards can also signify parts of your own personality that may be beneficial to you.

Combination of the Two Different Astrology Spreads

If you wish, you can combine both of the spreads. It can be very advantageous to lay the cards the first time around as an overall 12-month spread, and then on the second and following times, use the houses.

This is very good for answering questions such as:

What will my finances be like over the next 12 months?

What will my health be like over the next 12 months?

Your questions can be general for each area of your life. And you might want to do other spreads with more precise questions to examine each area in more detail.

No matter which way you use the spread, it is imperative to decide in advance what the positions will mean for you. When you do that, make your intents clear to your cards, and you will notice that the cards will always fall correctly for you.

And, when you decide what the positions will mean for you, stick with it. In other words, do not change your mind half way through the reading.

Identify Limiting Beliefs and Money Blocks Spread

This spread is intended to assist you in getting to the bottom of limiting beliefs and blockages regarding money. I would recommend that you give yourself sufficient time to work through each question and permit the answers to come to the surface from your intuition. You may notice that portions of your unconscious mind will perhaps attempt to stop you from answering these questions because those are the parts that want you to remain where you are.

Be sure you are comfortable and relaxed prior to starting. I would recommend that you grab a pen and piece of paper, and keep it with you as you do this. Also, have plenty of water for hydration.

As thoughts, feelings, emotions and beliefs arise, acknowledge them, and thank your subconscious for releasing them into your conscious awareness. Then, write them down.

You might choose to have your favorite energy-clearing tools close by in order to release any negative things that come up.

Be courageous and brave. Once certain things appear at the surface, feel through them and truly experience the energy of them. From that point on, it is your decision as to whether you will keep them or lovingly release them to the Universe.

It is wise to invite your angels, guides and the Higher Powers of the Universe to be with you to help.

If you find that something comes up that is too painful and tough to deal with on your own, stop the process and pursue proper professional help.

How to Lay Out the Cards

1) Your cards will be laid out by 3 rows of 3 cards, beginning at the top left, so you have 9 cards. Each of the cards has a question devoted to it.

2) Having read those 9 cards, put a 2nd layer of 3 rows of 3 cards on top of the 1st layer so that the cards beneath are concealed. These will also have a precise question devoted to them.

3) Now, move the cards in the 2nd layer off of the 1st layer so that the cards now sit side by side. This will give you 3 rows of cards that have 6 cards in each row or 9 sets of 2 cards.

4) Read the sets of cards, so that you now have 2 questions collected for each group. This is where you are going to begin to see the inconsistencies in

relation to your deep-seeded beliefs and your present
actions.

Protect Your Energies

When you begin to increase your energy vibration, you have a tendency to develop a bigger sensitivity to the negative energies surrounding you, and you may frequently find yourself taking on the negative energies of others or the negative situations surrounding you.

Ponder this for a moment. Have you ever felt really high on life, positive, full of confidence and ready to conquer the world? And then, suddenly, you come into contact with somebody who is unhappy, down on themselves and just simply dragging through every minute of every day.

Do you notice that it doesn't take long before you also feel down and unhappy, and your cheerfulness has faded?

Well, you just came into contact with an energy vampire, one who drained all your positive energy.

Be wary of the negative doom and gloom mongers and dream stealers who will give you tons of reasons why your plans are doomed. Don't let them in.

As you continue to work more with energies, it is important that you learn to protect your positive energies. Most negative individuals don't even grasp that they are draining the energy out of others. However, there are also individuals who intentionally set out to dispose of their flow of negative energies to others with the intent to cause harm or upset their balance in some way.

Below I have included some very easy techniques that you can use to protect yourself and your loved ones. Most of them contain visualization and some involve the use of crystals, color and mirrors.

1. Angels or Universe as Protectors

Call upon your angels to protect you or even your belongings. I often use this technique with my car while I am away on vacation. What I do is imagine that my angels are policemen with large clubs and guard dogs defending my property.

2. White Light

I also do this often. I imagine myself wrapped in a vast bubble of white light. Go ahead, try it. Imagine it is all around you, together with your feet and head, and notice it stretching around 3-4 feet past your own body.

And, here's a variation on this: imagine a cross of white light. Lure it in with your hands from top to bottom, left to right. Then, loop your hands around yourself like a corkscrew or whirlpool.

Once you've done that, imagine a green light all around you for healing and then add a purple light over the top for added protection.

3. Golden Light

Surrounding yourself in a bubble of golden light is even more powerful, because it permits love and virtuous things into your energy field and changes negative energy into positive energy, thereby returning it to the original sender as positive energy and love.

4. Dark Blue Cloak

Envision yourself inside a dark blue cloak. It completely surrounds you reaching down to the floor. Visualize wrapping it around your whole body and zipping up the hood so you are totally inside.

5. Shield

You can envision yourself with a shield around you. I visualize mine expanding up or coming down to the music from my favorite bank. This will put you inside and protected from anything negative. Yet, you can still communicate with others and are not closed off to everyone. You just simply do not take on any negative energies.

6. Crystals

If you are working on your computer either at home or work, set a piece of quartz by your side. It will absorb a lot of unwanted negative energies.

7. Tigers Eye

One of the most powerfully-known crystal shields is called Tigers Eye. In fact, it has been known for its protection qualities all the way back to the earliest times. You can carry it around with you, or you could envision it as one more coat of protection around you.

If you are going to use crystals, it is significant to wash them prior to use, preferably in salt water, allow them to dry in natural light and the charge them with the intentions of what you would like them to do - whether it be either healing or protection or both.

8. The Blue Flame of St. Germain

A very effective cleanser of negative energies is the Blue Flame of St Germain. This is a very special one, because it consumes any negative energy and transforms it into positive. Visualize yourself stepping into the flames. Also, you can wave your Tarot Cards through the flames to cleanse them of negative   energies.

These are just a few ways to protect your energies. It is important that you be positive, protect your energies and do not let others pull you down.

Be Your Own Life Coach using Tarot Cards

You know now that a Tarot reading can be beneficial to find out what is going on in your life and what the expected outcome might be of any given situation.

However, Tarot cards can offer so much more insight and direction than simply a traditional reading.

Tarot cards can lead you through a comprehensive coaching process, to guide you through a crisis to empowered decision making, where you are able to effectively take control of the situation and move it in the exact direction that you want it to go.

Here are some ways in which Tarot cards can be beneficial to you:

You can use Tarot cards to understand a situation, who might be involved and what has happened. It can be advantageous to ask questions starting with What? Who? When? And Where? For many individuals, the main question is 'why did this happen?' But that is not always the most productive question to ask at this point. A more suitable question might be "How did this happen?

Tarot cards can at that time be used to discover the root source of the situation in more detail. It is vital to perform this phase with as little fault or blame as probable. There might be a need to have some acceptance of the situation as it stands and the individuals involved. It has happened, you can't change it, so how can you move forward?

You can use your Tarot cards to recognize your true emotional state, feelings, inspirations and doubts and those of the other individuals involved.

The next area where Tarot cards can be valuable is to look at the possible consequences of the situation if nothing changes. Keep in mind that nothing is immovable. You have all control over decisions, actions and the direction your life will move in. As soon as you make a different decision or think differently, the whole reading changes.

You can consider and think about what the ideal outcome would be for you in the situation.

Ask of yourself what is stopping that from happening? This may be the situation or other individuals. It might also be innate fears and views about yourself or life overall. The Tarot can aid you in quickly identifying those issues and, once identified, they can be cleared with some easy exercises.

Use the Tarot for empowered decision making to discover some likely answers and look at the plausible outcomes of taking those steps, together with the likely reactions of other individuals.

Always take a deep breath, connect with your intuition, and recognize what feels right for you as a course of action.

Use your Tarot cards to confirm your intuitive state of mind.

And then, take action.

While you may want other individuals to change their behavior and actions in order to resolve the situation, that may not always happen. Others have their own agenda. Tarot cards can be most beneficial when you discover yourself and what you can do to change a situation and then take vested action.

Become your own life coach using Tarot cards to help you connect to your own inner guidance and obtain answers that are perfect for you – then take ACTION!

How to use Your Tarot Cards to Help You in Life and Business

Learning to read your Tarot cards for yourself can be an extremely valued ability in both life and business. It is significant to appreciate how Tarot cards can be used to help you and also what their limits are.

There are 3 chief areas in life and business where using Tarot cards can be very valuable to you.

They are:

1) Using info regarding different **Personality Archetypes** (shown below) to better appreciate yourself and others.

2) Personal growth, including developed intuition and inspiration, together with meditation skills, and

3) Realizing possible impending outcomes and using the cards for vested decision making.

Personality Archetypes

There are more than a few very diverse personalities that you will find in the Major Arcana and the Court Cards of the 4 suits. And, you will also find that we have added character traits and personality types when looking at reversed cards.

When working with or for an authoritarian, rule-driven, neurotic Emperor-type individual, you will have a very different experience as opposed to the tender, spur-of-the-moment, playful, plentiful Empress. A High Priestess sort of individual is expected to be extremely secretive and possibly very devious. You really don't want to experience working for a Devil personality!

From the 4 suits of Cups, Wands, Pentacles and Swords, we have 4 very diverse kinds of individuals. They range from the sensitive and delicate Creatives (Cups) to the action-oriented, Achievers (Wands) to the rational Communicators (Swords) and the hands-on Organizers (Pentacles), with endless combinations in between.

Tarot cards can be so advantageous for making sure that you have the correct individuals doing the correct jobs, so that they are working with their gifts and strengths.

Understanding the gifts and weaknesses of these archetypes can give you inordinate vision into the rudimentary character traits of the individuals in your work and personal life.

It can also be enormously valuable to perceive how they are behaving in the moment and how they are expected to respond in different circumstances and with different individuals.

If you are using Tarot cards to understand other people, then you can confirm what you see by the use of other things such as Astrology, Name Analysis and Numerology and/or other conventional personality assessment systems.

Personal Growth

When used for personal growth, Tarot cards can be a valuable connection to personal coaching. You can ask very detailed questions about yourself, your inspirations, your worries and your present circumstances.

The more explicit you are with your questions, the more perceptive the cards will be in helping you move forward in life.

Take a deep breath, relax and tap into your insight and internal wisdom, and you will know with laser-sharp precision when something is right or wrong.

By using Tarot cards to tap into your intuition, you can confirm your feelings as to what the exact ensuing steps are for you.

Through the Tarot cards, you are able to find your exact thoughts, feelings, passions, worries, fears, hopes, desires and actions or non-actions that you may or may not be applying to your problems/goals.

Tarot can be extremely revealing regarding what may be stopping you from being as fruitful as you would like with a plan or a goal.

The cards will disclose whether it is something that is outside of you and therefore out of your control, or whether it is something within you.

There may be beliefs about yourself or the world lying in wait beneath the surface, which are obstructive. Tarot cards are perfect for seeing through these blocks, both internal and external. The main blocks are more than likely in letting accomplishment, money, contentment and love to flow into your life. Very regularly the cards will also show the ways to overcome these blocks.

Future Outcomes and Empowered Decision Making

A Tarot card reading gives you the overall outcome of the way's things are developing, but that is if you do not make any changes to the way you are thinking, feeling or acting. And, remember that the cards assume that you aren't making any changes.

There is not much in our lives that is classified as fixed. We all possess free will in our selections, choices and actions. At times, things are going to hit you without warning, nevertheless you can, at all times, choose how to react.

If the outcome is looking somewhat challenging, you have the chance to make deviations, so that you can direct your life toward a more constructive path.

I would always recommend seeing the light at the end of the tunnel when life looks dim, drab and hopeless. Doing this will bring some anticipation, hopefulness and reassurance to your life. Frequently that will be sufficient to open up your own internal resources such as inspiration, problem solving, insight and the capability to notice a different way forward.

Contemplate an "alternate future" to the one which is presently unfolding and make improved, more knowledgeable choices. You can look for numerous possibilities to produce the future you want, and also look at ways of empowering you to get to where you truly want to go.

Having all of this knowledge under your belt, you can then make the most-informed choices and decisions. The cards will make you conscious of possible positives and trials in each path. Tarot cards do not make decisions for you. Only you can do that!

What Tarot Can't Do for You

Tarot cards will not tell you categorically what will happen in your life, and this is because you have ultimate control over which direction you go.

The cards can't provide you with explicit advice and the can't make decisions for you. They can't "make" you do anything.

They will not offer you immovable or unchangeable things, and it is extremely doubtful that they will foresee death, doom and devastation (and other things you can't do anything about) aside from worrying about their arrival.

There is nothing to be afraid of, as it is merely a deck of image cards. The power lies in the interpretation of the reading and the reputable standing that is given to the individual performing the interpretation.

Tarot cards are completely subjective, and everybody will see the cards in a different way.

Tarot has nothing at all to do with any religion, weird cults, devil worshipping, sorcery, voodoo or any other odd, silly thing.

You don't have to possess any distinct skills and you don't have to be a natural intuitive, medium or psychic to work with the cards.

How to Ask Questions to Get the Best Results Out of Your Tarot Cards

If you have a complicated decision to make, or are questioning whether you should trust somebody, Tarot cards can be a great help.

They can help you to swiftly access your insight and all your internal resources to help you to make the best choices. It is very probable that you already recognize the answer in your heart.

If you can feel it, it might be that you are questioning your instinct, and the cards will confirm your awareness or gut instinct.

First, remember to take a few deep breaths to relax and calm your mind and then ask your question. Ask that all of your answers be for the "highest and greatest good of all concerned".

Yes/No Questions

The most regularly asked questions are those needing a yes or no answer, such as:

- Will I get the job?
- Will he/she ask me out on a date?
- Should I move?
- Is my daughter/son become successful?
- Should I get married?

These questions can be very difficult to answer due to the fact that they have a fundamental assumption that our lives are mapped out for us, that everything is predetermined by somebody or something and that we have little or no impact over it.

This is not the case, as we all have free will and make our own decisions.

There might be circumstances that appear in our lives, over which we think we have no control. However, we can always elect how we react to them.

Power Questions

You want to be careful when attempting to answer a yes/no question. In fact, it might be more advantageous to ask questions such as:

- What would be the likely outcome if I did this or that?
- What do I need to know to make a decision about?
- What would most help me to move forward in this situation?
- How can I improve the communication between me and ...?"

The most powerful questions you can ask are about what you can personally do about a specific situation. What actions can you take? What decisions could you make? How could you change your feelings or reactions about something?

When you ask about the outcome of any given situation, keep in mind that the cards will provide you with a probable outcome IF you remain on precisely the same path and you do not make any variations. The cards assume that you are not going to change anything. Nevertheless, as soon as you do something in a different way, the whole shebang will change. This can be very valuable for looking at alternative prospects.

So, you could ask questions such as:

- What would the outcome be if I took the job I have been offered?
- What would be the outcome if I stayed in my current job?
- What would be the outcome if I applied for a promotion?"

Look at the various probable outcomes, and then make the choice that is best for you.

When you ask questions, it is vital to keep in mind that you can't change the behavior of somebody else, and it can be hard to get info about another individual because they may change their mind and do something totally different.

The clearer you are about what you want to know, the easier it will be to get a meaningful answer and some supportive direction.

Trust Your Immediate Response

Pull 2 or 3 cards (or however many seem appropriate to you) and trust that the answers will be the correct one's.

Notice what you see, the colors, symbols and images are on the cards, notice everything that pops out of the cards at you. Be conscious of any instantaneous feelings, thoughts, words or impressions.

Take note of your instant reaction. Trust it. That is what is going to provide you with the clearest answers. When you start to rationally analyze the card, then the power of that innate prompt can quickly be lost.

Look up meanings if you would like some extra perceptions or distinctions, though I would strongly recommend that you don't do that since you might weaken the power of the answers that have come from your own unconscious mind or higher self or inner wisdom.

Remember that you are the one in control, and the Tarot is simply a tool in your toolbox.

Develop Your Intuition Through Tarot

Tarot cards can be a great way to advance your insight and give you the self-confidence to trust your intuition.

In an ideal world, you want to get to a place where your intuition automatically kicks in every time you need it and you don't have to even think about it.

You just know when something is right or wrong and you trust it entirely.

Tarot can also help you safely discover possible opportunities prior to committing yourself to making a decision and can provide you with guidance in any area of your life.

The Power of Images

Your mind thinks in images, and the Tarot contains 78 color images and symbols, many of which are very ancient, which means they are one of the most powerful ways of connecting directly with your intuitive mind.

Images are the first form of teaching and learning, because they tell stories and go right to the right side of your brain, which is all about inspiration, thoughts, creativity, ideas and visions.

The images, colors and symbols speak directly to your intuitive mind to provide you with answers that are accurate for you. This is why different individuals can look at the same cards and give a different explanation because the cards speak to everybody individually.

Intuition is like any muscle. The more you use it, the more it will work for you when you need it.

The Tarot is one of the fastest ways to develop our intuition or gut instinct and have it available all the time for whenever we need to make an important decision.

Relaxation and Breathing

Relaxation and breathing techniques will benefit you greatly in your quest to become the best Tarot reader you can be. Find a quiet spot where you won't be bothered and sit comfortably.

Take a few deep breaths. Breathe out any strain and tension from your day. Breathe in self-confidence and   harmony.

A useful breathing exercise: breathe in to the count of 7, hold your breath for 7, gradually release to the count of 7, and hold for 7. Repeat as many times as necessary.

Once you feel tranquil and calm, pick up your deck of cards and shuffle them. A good question to ask would be:

"What would be most beneficial to know about my situation right now?"

When ready, stop shuffling, cut the cards, spread out in front of you and select one. Take note of your initial thoughts, feelings and impressions.

Sights, Sounds and Feelings

What words do you hear? What is the manner and volume of the voice? Is it inside of your head or outside of you?

What feelings do you get when you look at the card? Where in your body are those feelings?

Where are the images, inside your head, or in front of you? Are they color or black and white, still or moving?

Are there any sensations in your body, and if so, where are they?

Do you get any images flashing through your mind?

Those initial answers will most likely be the right ones for you, so trust them.

You don't want to stare at the card for too long because your rational mind will undoubtedly begin to analyze and might end up judiciously talking you out of accepting those initial perceptions.

Once you learn to recognize the signs that your instinct is using to connect with you, you can recognize them more rapidly in another situation.

With a bit of practice, you will quickly differentiate between the answers from your insight and the logic of your critical mind.

Both are significant, and the critical mind can be very valuable once you have collected all of your creative intuitions.

Then, when ready, relax, still your mind and pick another card.

Build Up the Story

Put a couple of cards side by side and take note of the impressions that you get. Notice how the story begins to change when one card is following another.

Keep a "Tarot Journal", where you can write down any visions that come from your Tarot card deck.

Once you have documented your individual wisdom, you could then read up more on the Tarot to see if there are any other distinctions that can be added. Though, keep in mind that the meanings in other books are the views of those authors and might refute your own perceptions.

Overall, once you have practiced much, certain cards will come to have specific meanings for you. These might be very unlike other definitions you find in a book, and that is okay. Actually, that is perfect. Use what you feel is right for you with each individual card.

The messages you receive from your inner senses will be the accurate ones for you personally, so it is vital that you follow those first.

You will begin to grow a connection with your cards and eventually trust them completely as a tool to access your insight whenever you want and need it.

The Art of Storytelling Through Tarot Card Reading

There are an overabundance of books and articles about reading Tarot cards and many of them oppose each other. When you are just starting out learning to read, this can be very perplexing. You can get caught up in wondering which interpretation is the "correct one."

Honestly, there is no correct one.

The images on Tarot cards tell a story making them a great way to connect with your higher self, because images are the first method of learning and can make a direct connection with your unconscious mind. Because the Tarot is individual to everybody, this is why you get very diverse viewpoints on each card.

As you practice, each card will mean something specific to you. Notwithstanding that, you can still unexpectedly get an instinctual flash as you look at a card, and it might mean something that it has not meant before.

It is important to build your own relationship with your cards and develop your own explanations.

When you have selected a deck of Tarot cards, remove a card from the deck.

You can begin with the Fool card, the first card of the Major Arcana. Or you can pick a card randomly. It does not matter.

Notice the colors and symbols, as well as any direct feelings that you get when you look at the card.

Does it remind you of somebody?

Do you find yourself thinking of a specific situation?

Do you relate to the circumstances in the image?

Now, take another card and take a good look at it. Observe. Lay it next to the other card and notice how the story changes.

As you look at the 2 cards together, build up a story of what is happening. How have things changed from one card to the other?

Just envision that you are telling a story to a child, and use the images to arouse your intuition.

It's not imagination, and you are not just making things up, so never let anyone tell you that. The Tarot is a powerful way for your intuition to connect with you or the person you are reading.

When reading for somebody else, simply describe to them what you see going on in the images, and you will be astonished at how precise the reading is. It might not make much sense to you, but your customer's subconscious mind will take your words together with the visual of the image and create the precisely correct message for them.

Then add another card and continue the story. A reading based on 3 cards is one of the easiest spreads. It is frequently used as a Past/Present/Future situation, while it doesn't need to be.

Learn How to Read Tarot Cards by Looking at the Colors and Pictures

Color plays a substantial role in your deck of cards, especially in the Rider Waite Tarot deck.

The main colors of each card have an instant effect on your senses, how you feel about that particular card and any messages that your awareness may be trying to provide to you.

When you draw a card, take a minute and have a look at it. Take note of the colors and notice how the card makes you feel. The very first response you get will be the correct one, so it is vital that you don't dismiss it.

Really look at the images. What is essentially happening in the card?

Does anything jump out at you?

Do you get any specific emotional state when you look at certain cards?

Do some cards give you an immediate good feeling or an immediate feeling of anxiety?

Take note of any observations that you make in your Tarot Journal.

Yellow as a dominant color largely gives a positive, cheerful, sunshine feel to the card. This will regularly be related to your feelings and tour outward expression of things.

Red as the strongest color will frequently point to material things and matters having to do with the outside world.

There are quite a few cards with Blue as the predominant color, and this is frequently related to matters of heart, the inner self and intuition.

A dominance of Green specifies things to do with the earth and nature.

White is color of purity, virtue and light. Cards with a dominance of white will encompass significant messages in relation to your spiritual side.

There are some cards which are very dark in color or have a predominance of **Black** in them. Sometimes, these cards can cause a momentary brief fear. The color black can have different meanings in diverse cultures. In some, it is sign of death. In others, it is a sign of rebirth and new beginnings. In others, it is a sign of power.

Grey is customarily linked with wisdom and old age.

Colors also relate to the energy centers or chakra points in our bodies. Each of the colors and chakra points have a different meaning and are related to our interpretations of the Tarot cards.

How to Shuffle Your Tarot Cards for Best Results

Prior to doing a reading, shuffle your deck of cards to make sure that any energies from earlier readings have been cleared, and then give the cards to your client to shuffle.

The reason for doing this is so you can make a connection with the cards so that your energy is in them.

While shuffling, think about what you want the cards to help you with. And ask your client to do the same. The better you phrase the question, the clearer the answer will be.

Be sure that your cards are all the right way up prior to beginning the reading. That way if any end up reversed, it will be significant for that particular reading and not just a leftover reversed card from a former reading.

There are a couple of ways you can shuffle your cards:

1. Hold then upright and shuffle them like playing cards.
2. Put them on the surface in front of you facing down, and mix them up however feels the most comfortable to you.

Shuffle for as long as feels right for you.

If a card is to fly out while shuffling or you drop a couple of cards, it is because they are expected to be significant to the reading. Take a look, and note what they are. If you are reading for somebody else and they are shuffling, ask them to see what the card is, and make note of it. It might appear in a prominent place in the reading. If not, then it was simply a matter of slippery cards.

Put the card back, and continue shuffling.

If you drop all of the cards, pick them up without looking and carry on.

Put them all back together in 1 pile, with the pictures facing down.

With your left hand, cut the deck into 3 piles. Customarily, you will use the hand that you don't write with. So, if you are left-handed, you would use your right hand and vice versa. This is so you have less control over that hand, and you will be more likely to allow in the inspiration of your unconscious mind.

Cut the cards 2X so that you have 3 piles, and then put them back together as 1 pile.

Then take the cards off of the top of the pile and use for the reading.

Prepare Yourself and Your Tarot Cards Before Every Reading

Prior to beginning any reading, it is vital to be sure that the energies of the preceding reading are cleared from your cards and from your space.

There are several ways you can do this:

- Wave the cards through incense or sage to clear them to shuffle, and ask that all old energies be released.
- Light a candle in the space you are going to use.
- Spray some cleansing essences around the room.
- Envision the Blue Flame of St Germain, which is used a lot for clearing. This is a blue flame that consumes everything negative and turns it into positive.

Before beginning any reading, it is also imperative to make sure you are ready and in the most open frame of mind.

If you can't fully let go of your own troubles, it might be advantageous to visualize that you are putting them in a wooden box and closing the lid firmly. Your worries can stay there until after the reading.

You can cleanse your own energies in the same way that you cleanse your cards. Also, deep breathing works very well. As you breathe out, release all negativity, and as you breathe in, fill yourself up with light and peace.

Ground yourself by imagining roots coming out of your feet and going deep down into the Earth. Then connect yourself up to the Universe so that you are drawing in light and energy.

You can also ask your angels and guides to bring you the info you need from a place of the highest love, truth and rightfulness and that what is coming through is for the highest good of all concerned. Trust in that

And, always remember to thank your angels, guides and helpers when you have finished the reading.

The more peaceful you are when you are doing a Tarot card reading, the clearer and more useful the answers will be that you are receiving.

Reversals

Some individuals use reversals. Others don't.

Some folks totally disregard reversed cards and look at them like they are simply upright. Some make it so there are always reversed cards in the reading. The choice is yours, and you will know better as you go along.

I have a tendency to make sure that all of the cards are in the upright position. If a reversed card appears, then it is most likely because it is what is meant to happen, and there is a significant message coming from it.

Sometimes a client will shuffle the cards by mixing them up through some elaborate card-splitting. That being the case, there might be many reversed cards, and sometimes it can be tough to know which way should be upright. Then it becomes a matter of instinct to know which cards look to be relevant.

Notice what feels right or not to you.

Work with the reversed cards the same way that you would an upright card. Take note of how the picture is now different. Ask what is now happening? Is there anything that is more prominent in the reversed position? Look at the colors, shapes, symbols and how things now relate to each other in the reversed position. Does something stand out more than it did earlier?

See how the card makes you feel and any visions that come to mind. You might get an entirely different sensation from the card. Look at the reversed card with regard to the other cards around it. Take note of how it changes the image with those cards as well.

When a reversed card is important, it will have an effect on the other cards surrounding it. See the entire spread as a complete picture.

In the Rider Waite Smith Deck of Tarot Cards, the cards are very graphic with clear images which can be a very valuable trigger to your intuition when the cards are in the reversed positions.

If reversals do not happen very often in your readings, it is perhaps more effective to use your intuition to decide the meaning in the situation that it has shown up instead of trying to refer to a book for meanings.

Timing

A question that I'm often asked is about the "timing" of events and how this applies to the reading of Tarot cards. This is actually a hard question to answer due to the fact that our lives/life events are not immovable.

We've all heard the old saying "things happen in their own good time" or "events have a divine timing". Sometimes events transpire completely in their own way and on their own time.

It really all falls upon your vantage point as to whether you feel that there is a "divine force" that is directing the timing of events or whether we can control timing.

Most of us have, at some point, tried to control events and tried to force something to occur in a specific way and in a precise timeframe. Sometimes this works, sometimes not.

Sometimes I offer a six-month reading. Each layer of the spread represents a different month. I once did a reading for someone who was going through a difficult divorce. I provided her with an arrangement of events for the next 6 months. She called me approximately 3 weeks later and informed me that the entire sequence had occurred in about 2 weeks.

I think that the reason for that was because of a change in her own energy after the reading. She now knew that things were going to go in her favor, and that had provided her with the self-confidence to take a more proactive, forceful approach. In turn, that lead to the matter being resolved in 2 weeks rather than 6 months.

When individuals ask questions regarding timing, there is regularly a fundamental supposition that life is immovable and that events are going to occur anyhow and there is not much we can do about it.

This is seen in questions such as:

- When will I get married?
- Will I change jobs?
- How many children will I have?
- When will I move?

The answers to questions such as these are frequently determined by the actions that somebody either does take or does not take with regard to the matter at hand.

For example, if somebody asks, "When will I change jobs?" I would ask them whether or not they have been taking any action in the direction of changing jobs. If not, then I would want to know if there is anything surrounding their work that is going to cause a change in employment. If not, then it is expected that their job will remain the same until they do something on their own to change it.

Questions of timing sometimes also come up when somebody very much wants something to occur, but the outcome might be determined by somebody else. This is often seen when an individual is in a love-triangle with somebody but that individual is currently married to somebody else. Your customer will very badly want the cards to say that the love of their life will be leaving their spouse soon.

It doesn't matter how they phrase that question, they are not likely to get the answer they want because of timing. It is ultimately determined by other people's actions.

Sometimes individuals will ask when something is going to happen. They ask this type of question when they are in inside of a situation and they want to know how things are unfolding or when a definite event is going to happen or not happen.

Sometimes this is easier to see, because the cards might specify things moving forward quickly and favorably for somebody. There might be many wands cards, specifically the 8 of Wands or favorable cards such as the 10 of Cups or the 6 of Wands or The Star Card or World Card. This may mean a favorable outcome is forthcoming.

There is a very solid flow of positive energy in the cards.

You can find out if things appear to be not moving forward which could be because of the individual themselves or outside influences. The individual might not be prepared to make a choice and move forward. You can regularly see why a specific occurrence is not moving forward and what your customer might be able to do about it. Sometimes it is merely a change in attitude or a different choice or a different method on the part of your customer that can make an enormous difference.

I have often noticed this situation with positive prospects which are trying to come to an individual but nothing is occurring since that individual is not open to receiving them.

The timing of events is often determined by the energy of the person being read. Change can occur on the spot, but attempting to put a precise time on something can for the most part be counter-productive. If your customer wants something to happen, they perhaps want the result right now instead of in a few weeks, so it might be best for you to tell them to look at their views and attitudes to see what obstructions they might want to get rid of in order to lure in their wanted outcome.

When somebody asks you about timing, it may be beneficial to find out whether they have thoughts of "It is all charted out and there is nothing I can do about it" or "I can produce the timing of events in my life" and then adapt the reading accordingly.

Conclusion

By using your Tarot cards in any of the ways explained above, or combined together, your Tarot cards will become your friend. You will possess a very powerful tool for tapping into your incredibly powerful inner resources of self-understanding, instinct, intuition, creativity and problem-solving.

Tarot is a remarkable tool both enjoyment and personal development. Just like anything in this world, it can be used for helpful, great things or it can be used for negative, damaging disempowerment.

That decision lies with the individual who is reading the cards. It is my sincere hope that you are the former.

It is a wonderful opportunity to take control of your life and make much-needed changes, before life decides to make them for you.

Blessings to you and yours...

He who asks is a fool for five minutes, but he who does not ask remains a fool forever.

- Chinese Proverb

228

If you enjoyed learning how to read tarot, I would be forever grateful if you could leave a review. Reviews are the best way to give newer authors like myself feedback. They also help out your fellow readers find the books worth reading so make sure to help them out!

Printed in Great Britain
by Amazon